Resilience in Hard Times
Anthology

RESILIENCE IN HARD TIMES ANTHOLOGY

Paulette Harper

THY WORD PUBLISHING
CALIFORNIA

Published by Thy Word Publishing

Antioch, CA 94531

2021 Paulette Harper

Book Cover Design: Tywebbin Creations

Interior Book Design & Formatting: https://tywebbincreations.com

Editor: Paulette Nunlee https://fivestarproofing.com

Library of Congress Cataloging-in-Publication Data

ISBN-13: 978-1-7370931-0-7

Published and printed in the United States of America.

CONTENTS

ACKNOWLEDGMENTS

My thoughts are filled with beautiful words for the king,
and I will use my voice as a writer would use pen and ink.
(Psalm 45:1 CEV)

To every person on my team who worked with me to bring this vision to reality with excellence.

Everyone who prayed for me, the co-authors, and this project.

Special thanks to the readers everywhere who have supported this project. You have many books to choose from. Thank you for adding *Resilience in Hard Times* to your library.

To the Resilience in Hard Times contributing authors, you did it. You should be proud of yourself for this great accomplishment.

And most importantly, my Lord and Savior, Jesus Christ. This could not have happened without You.

Thank You for using my gift to be a blessing to others and to use it for Your glory. I am reminded everyday of Your favor and blessings on my life. You continue to open up doors of opportunity for me to share my gift to the world. As I continue to write and open the doors for other writers, may what we pen always be inspired by the Holy Spirit. You continue to do great things for me.

FEATURED SPONSOR - TONYA BARBEE

I ALMOST MADE MY RESIDENCE THE MENTAL WARD

Prince Charming had on a shiny, silver, suit with a paisley tie and white shirt. Ok, back then, those suits were stylish. He looked professional, as if he just left a "good government job," as my dad would say. He made his way over to me. We never stopped looking at each other. He reached over to my right ear and told me his name. I loved his voice too. He was my future husband. We danced all night.

Within a year, he proposed. He had already moved in with me and my young son. He made me smile. He spoiled us. I was always laughing at his jokes. He helped around the apartment. I was grateful to have him in our lives.

We planned the small wedding, which was held at a beautiful, quaint, church in D.C. We invited all of our family.

As I walked down the aisle towards him, I had this strong urge to run the opposite way. I squeezed my uncle's arm, as he gave me away, and kept walking towards my future husband while watching the smiling faces of our guests.

Within a year, we had our first, baby girl. Shortly afterward, he got a promotion to sales executive and we built our dream home. I felt we were in a great place, happy. Before long, he was traveling for his job. He was never home, only home long enough to repack. I discovered I was pregnant again. He demanded that I abort the baby. I refused and harbored resentment. He began to ridicule me for not making as much money as him. He became emotionally abusive. When he did speak to me he spat words at me as if I was an imposition. He ignored the kids and did not want to discuss the baby that was growing in my stomach. It became unbearable to live with him, but I was determined to save my marriage. Then during one business trip, I called him in his hotel room and a woman answered the phone. I hung up. That explained the frequent trips. I snapped.

I had planned to purchase a gun "after" my obstetrician appointment. He needed to die. How could he cheat on me? I took care of the kids, the house, held down a decent job, made love to him even when I was too tired, and looked good for him, even when I didn't feel good. How could he?

While visiting my doctor, he said, "baby is doing well." Then he asked me about my plans for the weekend. I smiled and told him, "I'm going to kill my husband when he gets back home." He put his warm hand on top of mine and asked me did I feel like taking a ride to the hospital. I told him, "Sure, I can take care of "this" later." I made one phone call to my girlfriend to get my kids for me and pick up my car. I was then sent by ambulance to a mental ward in Virginia. I was having a nervous breakdown.

When I arrived at the hospital, I was numb. I glared at the admitting nurse as she was asking me for my medical information. I handed over my purse and told her everything they needed was in there. Then the nurse came in smiling and asked me to follow her. I was told to remove my clothing and put on the hospital gown. I kept thinking about what I was going to do. Being right there at the front door sitting on the steps waiting for him as he arrived and then. Perfect opportunity. I did not care about living anymore. I tried everything. I loved him, my family, my job, everything. It was never enough. I could no longer stand the pain.

I eventually met with the psychiatrist. He told me I would get psychotherapy for an extensive period until I got better. I was unable to receive medication because I was in my second trimester.

My sister and young nephew came to visit after I had been

in the hospital for two days and he said to me, "Aunt Tonya, why are you in the hospital with the crazy people?" I looked around the recreation room, where we were sitting, and only then did I notice where I was. The patients were walking around like zombies. My sister, as she handed me my Bible, tried to hush my nephew as he kept asking me, but only then did I realize what was happening. I was in a mental ward and I needed to get better before this became my permanent place of residence. I became worried about my children and the one in my belly. My father, said to me, "Tonya, no one in our family has ever been in a mental ward before." My best coworker called me while I was making dog leashes for my pets and said, "Are you in the mental ward?" I told him, I was, and he was shocked. My closest friends and family prayed for me. I read my Bible, determined for change. The darkness I felt had to be removed. Ephesians 5:8 says, "For at one time you were darkness, but now you are the light in the Lord. Walk as children of light."

I stayed in the hospital for seven days. My husband wasn't worth me losing my mind over. I needed to be there for my kids. Who would have taken care of them? What I learned is when we snap, we can regain control of our minds with prayer, determination, and faith in God.

I made a decision not to kill my husband but to divorce him, focus on my faith, continue therapy when I left the hospital, and be there for my children. No one should have that kind of power over your life. Push through the pain to get to that better place. I decided not to stay in the mental ward and to get home to my children.

ABOUT THE AUTHOR

Tonya Barbee has served in the educational field all of her adult life. She earned her B.S. and M.B.A. at National-Louis University in Chicago, IL. She's been working for the federal government for over 35 years and the Founder of I am Still a Rose, LLC where she inspires and empowers those that want to move beyond whatever is holding them back. She also has inspiring apparel and other products for both men and women.

Tonya has been featured in "My LYFF Story," "Turning Up the Gospel," "Goodreads," "Joyous Word," Renee Wiggins' Blog Radio Show," "Push-it News," "Scoop USA Newspaper," Ernest Armstrong with "Say Your Peace" Radio, Jeff Foxx Radio, WBGR with Lionel Green, Daulton Anderson of WHCR, Cheryl Wood's of VOX Radio, Black News, Allison Daniels' Authors Chat with Allison Podcast, Queenie's Book Talk and Reviews and a host of others. Her published works are the Little Girl Inside and I am Still a Rose. She's also participated in two anthologies: Sharing Our Prayers and Joyfully in His Care. She's also a radio show host at WBGR, "the Still a Rose Show," and, has a podcast, "Barbee's Real Talk" and a member of Toastmasters, "Go Pro." She's an inspirational speaker and a dynamic coach, where she makes a difference. Tonya is also a member of the Eta Phi Beta Sorority, Epsilon Zeta Chapter.

She's a native of Durham, NC with four children, eight grandchildren. She is a member of First Baptist Highland Park Church in Landover, MD, officiated by Rev. Dr. Henry P. Davis, III, where she is active as well as in her community.

Connect with Tonya

www.tonyabarbee.com

RESILIENCE IN HARD TIMES
FOUNDING SUPPORTERS

PAULETTE HARPER

Annie Mae Mitchell

Agnes Heard

Angela Cutter

Anita Logan

Alexanderia Harris

Angela King

Annette & Donald Wright

Ashley Mix

Anthony Johnson

Alice Carrington

Amanda Moore

Ashley Nicole Williams

Andre Gamble

Angela Gary

Ava Thomas

Atari Starks

April Minger

Andretta Black

Aneatra Harvey

Angela Lovest

Antoine Isaac

Ariel Dews

Austin Dews

Berryl Martin

Barry Jerrels

Belinda and Charles Hooks

Brian Cooper

Billie Jiles

Bernadine Gamble-Sequeira

Beverly Briggs-Brice

Barbara Mcneal

Bobby Henderson

Beverly Allen

Cassie Vaughn

Clarence Shaw

Cadel Jackson

Chalfonte' Thompson

Cherise Primm

Cher Tuano

Claretta Bruns

Carlos Lopez

Cordell A. Zachery

Cordell I. Zachery

Chekita Griggs

Carla Preyer

Cheryl Robinson

Connie Cochell

Camelia Houston

Candace Bourgeois

Christina Shields

Chandra Legue

Candace Hunt

Charlotte Bayone

Christopher Jackson

Collette Charles

Cheronne Burks

Cheryl Turner

Cicely Jackson

Clarissa Quinn-Turner

Cassandra Gamblin

Cynthia Philpot

Chelsea Joseph Yates

Cheryl Roy Combs

Cindy & David Richardson

RESILIENCE IN HARD TIMES ANTHOLOGY

Dalzenia Williams

Deborah Hooks

Delphine Shaw

Daniel Parenti

Doris Coney-Pergues

Debra Wirth

DeLesa Swanigan

Denise Boyd

Doni Mabrie

Debbie Speese

Dr. Danita McCray

Dyhana Stewart

Debbie Haggin

Deborah Hudson

Deja Bradley

Dr. Gert Cooley

Daijha CJ Solomon

Darlene Wilkins

Deloris Del Finklea

Denise Zeigler

Donald P Williams

Danette Brown

Deborah Hill

De'Meatrice Hodges

Diedra Marien

DeLisa Oakley

Denise Beshears

Diana Bracy

Dianna Mostella-Greely

Dorries Oakley

Doreen Ransaw

Earl Warren

Erin Proctor

Estelle Mannion

Elisa Richardson

Eleanor Keys

Ebony Bowen

Erika Harris

Earnestine Oakley

Elaine Taylor

Evelyn Fuller

Ezekiel Fernandez

Edith Thompson

Elaine Crocker

Elizabeth Lugo

Ethel Lewis

Felicia Scott

Florence Newbill

Felicia Permmillion

Felicia Byrd

Francia Anderson

Floyd Gamble

Fritz Miller

Gigi Crowder

Gloria Paveljack

Genetia Roberts

Gwendolyn LeBrane

Gloria Barker

Paulette Harper

Helen Sledge

Herticene Davis

Henderson Family

Hazel Harris

Isabelle Anthony Ramos

Irene Bueno

Ifoma Erhabor

Janice Cutter

Jannie Williams

Jesse Dews

John White

Jessica Preston

John Callaway

Jaki Guilford

Jaclyn Richardson

Janaya Castain

Jeannie Dawson

Joannie Luke

Jovan Williams

James Wood

Jammaar Hall

Jeanette Taylor

Jonathan McCoy

Josh Kirwin

Joy Hunt

Jackie Spenser

Janice Williams

Jena Graham

Joette Garcia

Jeanette McLean

Jennifer Bush

Jackie Mungo

Jeannine Sawyer-Brown

Joseph Pete Yates

Joseph Taylor

Jay Wynn

Jacqueline Crooks

Jacqueline Morris

Pastor Jaron Heim

Jeneen Rainey-Tatum

Elder Joan Kirkling

Juanita Winbush

Kristen Panillio

Katoria Mitchell-Chanyasubkit

KeiSha Osgood

Keith Osgood

Kezia Allen

Kia Gamble

Karen Oslter

Karen Gentry

Karita Webber

Kieona Ballard

Ka'Misha Crittendon

Karen Torres

Kela Richardson

Kim Mayes-Bedford

KimWesley

Dr. Kimberly Stokes

Katherine Romar

Kathi Aldridge

Kristina Mathena

Kamaryn Roberts

Kanesha Gamble

Kimberlee Blakey

Kijana and Kyleigh Davis

Kathryn Toni

Kathy Mazzone

Keith Harris

Karen Early

Kandis Williams-Gallagher

Karyn Linder-Trussell

RESILIENCE IN HARD TIMES ANTHOLOGY

Lavone Mcgruder

Lisa Coney

LaTanya Nivins

Lena Zachery

Lyn Roberts

Laurie Parker

Loren & Sydney Adams

Landis Rush

Lisa Lopez

Lakesha Magee

Laura Galicha

Leondra Montgomery

Lakeisha Gilchrist

Laura Blane

Lauren Cain

Lessie English

Lossie Brown

Lula Harris

LaDonna Whitney-Alexander

Lana McKee

Latrice Gamblin-Joyce

Linda Belton

Lucindy Harrison

Lawrence Brooks

Linda McCray

Lillishia Stingley

Lois Williams

Larishia Johnson

LaSandra Edwards

LaVetta Coleman

Linda Williams

Lisa Carlson

Lolita Shirley

Lorraine White

Lynda Lee

Lynette Barnum

Maxine Emmanuel

Marilyn Coney

Monica Rucks

Michael and Ardella Vance

Mary Van

Monique James

Marthenia Satterfield

Michelle Stefin

Misty Clark

Maezola West-Dills

Mardeio Cannon

Mercedes Bowie

Maurice Golden

Maya Bulleit

Micaiah Wood

Marjory White

Marlon Gamble

Mashyia Gamble

Michele Plevin

Mary Berry

Melissa Nattiel

Melonese Martin

Marie Stith

Martha Fernandez

Michelle Stewart

Marcia Harris

Mark Max Beasley

Maudrie Daigle

Michelle Alexander

Myiah Watson

PAULETTE HARPER

Napat Napatwarang

Nina Jones

Nancy Carey

Nemsen Harris

Natasha McGee-Jones

Niccole Adams

Norma Lovelace

Nasan Tamika Fitz

Neotha Dryver

Nikysha Owens

Olga Whitten

Oris Harris

Pamela Bryant

Patricia Guillory

Pamela Page

Pamela Marsh

Patrina Dickens

Quinton J. Ross

Quanda Price

Regina Williams

Robert Henderson, Jr.

Ruthie Burts

Raymond Callaway

Ruby McBee

Regina Major

Robbie DeShay

Rosetta Nelson

Rossana Marvin

Randall Ogans

Ruth Richardson

Raven Johnson

Richard Baker

Robbie Peirce

Rosa Penns

Roxanne Mcclellan

Ralonda Davis

Rina Stefani

Rose Reither

Reshanda Gamble

Robert Jackson

Roderick Fields

Ron Rocketman

Ryan Lockner

RESILIENCE IN HARD TIMES ANTHOLOGY

Symone Hurt

Sabrina Henderson

Stephani Walton

Sara Booker

Sarah Hoving

Sharon Kelly

Shirley Bearden

Shirley Reid

Staci Johnson

Sue McCarty

Sabrina Sobye

Satin Howard

Sharron Hubbard

Sherrita Carter

Sheya Chisenga

Susan Schultz

Shawnteia Yeargin

Sovereign Grace

Selena Feathers

Shavonne Hollowell

Sherry Beasley

Staci Banks-Lightfoot

Safi Wright

Shavia Johnson

Silvia Carter

Sandra McKoy

Sheena Van Zyl

Sharon Lucas

Steve Lesler

Sue Violette

Simone Gamble

Sonia Freytes

Skye Davis

Skye Burgman

Traci Harris

Travis Greene

Tanya Johns

Terry Williams

Trudi Johnson

Terri Johnson

Tishouna Brown

Toi Heim

Toyin Spencer

Tracy Lewis

Tamara Allen

Tomye Aldridge

Tatlin Brickman

Toni CollyPerry

Tony Davis

Tonya Donald

Tycee Gamble

Tina Banks-Cox

Teresa Felix

Tiquilla Simpson

T.R. Harris

Tracy McCoy

Travis Gardner

TreShawn Harris

Twame Gaddy

Twana Hendrix

Treasure Davis

Valerie Samuels

Vallierie Lawson

Valerie Thrash

Vanessa Crumble

Valerie McCoy

Verta Clark

Venia Royston

Vern Felix

Valynne Williams

Venita Cowlah

Vera Quiwa

Virginia Paul Fuller

William Brown

Willie Brown, Jr.

Wanda Price

Willie McCoy

Wanda Kelly

Waylen Williams

Wendell Williams

Wesley Cook

Yvonne Roberts

Yvette Sanders

Yolanda Thomas

PRAISE FOR RESILIENCE IN HARD TIMES

"Each narrative defines a pivotal and jarring moment that compels the authors to activate their faith at a greater level and propelled them into living a purpose-driven life filled with God's abundant blessings and valuing the God in them." – *Marie S. Hall*

"In this powerful and aptly titled collection of writings, twenty resilient women share accounts of betrayal, hurt, and healing. Moving through pain, stepping out on faith and trusting God through loss are running themes throughout this book and I am definitely here for all of it!" – *Cassietta Jefferson, Author and Blogger*

"Their testimonies will promote and engender healing for everyone dealing with similar events. Each of the twenty stories relate a personal hard time and how they struggled and worked diligently to get a handle on their often heart-rending circumstance. For those who are going through a mild rough patch or a calamity, these wonderful essays are sure to shine through your despair.

Especially recommended as a gift." – *Lisa Lickel, lisalickel.com, Author of UnderStory and UnderCut*

"As I read each story, I felt I knew them, because small parts of their stories I could truly relate to. Because I have experienced parts of their journey or knew someone who had. This book helps you to know you're not alone in the struggle and not alone in the victory. This is a much read." – *Shurvone Wright, Author/Speaker/Social Media Business Strategist*

"Words of female warriors. Fighters. Ladies who will not take no for an answer. This is how I would describe what I found in-between the pages of *Resilience in Hard Times*. Stories from the everyday woman that has been in a time where it seems that things were not in their favor, but they overcame it." – *Patrice, SCBookGal843*

"Harper's introductory essay, "*Resilience While Waiting,*" offers the ballast needed for the entries to follow. These heartfelt stories—while outlining times of struggle—also emphasize the value of resilience and offer affirmations based on Scripture.

The value of such a collection is that, as a reader, all of my emotions are engaged. While being sympathetic regarding the experiences contained within the pages, I'm also energized by the spiritual takeaways. Everyone faces hard times; the key is how you choose to handle them."– *Amy Wilson for Novels Alive*

"There was something in every story that took me back to some painful episodes that happened in my very own life. This book is an absolute must-read for anyone that is depressed, overwhelmed, suffering from low self-esteem, or all the above. If you need stronger faith, then you must read *Resilience in Hard Times*." – *Dr. Kathleen B. Oden*

"I enjoyed reading stories from these twenty women who learned how to survive and pivot in the most troubling times, many of which left me in tears. *Resilience in Hard Times* was one exciting read." – *Arlena Dean*

"The moment you decided to share your story another woman could breathe. You are taking a moment from your lives and saying to us look at what happened and look how I made it out."– *Pastor Cynthia Robinson*

"I encourage you to sit and breathe and allow Holy Spirit to take your hand and walk with you through the pages of *Resilience in Hard Times*. And set aside any predisposed comparisons in your mind or heart and tune your ears to the life-giving whisper of God resounding through the testimonies you are about to read. I was able to relate to many of them and felt the strength of God rushing on my soul like soothing waters of reassurance, healing, unspeakable mighty hope, and mercy from the Most High God." – *Dr. Emiko Flores*

"Love, Love, this book! Yes, this book is written with much honesty and clarity. The authors are transparent about their life experiences, and they will take you on an amazing journey from pain to triumph. You will see how God will step right in and will deliver you from whatever circumstance you may be facing that isn't lined up with His will. I have found myself ministered to through this book. Life does bring us some challenges that can take us down a dark path, but only God can heal us and set us free."– *Donna Moses, Co-Author, Arise From The Ashes*

"*Resilience in Hard Times* is about courage, strength, endurance, faith, and the ability to persevere in difficult times and moments of adversity. Wow, this book is about real-life stories of trials and the power to triumph over situations that were mean to harm us physically, mentally, or emotionally. We have all been there and what I liked about the book was that through every story, it was as if the author was taking a page out of my personal life story." – *Debbie Renee Howard, Brilliance Coach*

"*Resilience in Hard Times* is a quick read that introduces a global collaboration of twenty authors sharing their diverse lifetime experiences. The raw truthful collection of stories of their journeys wring a variety of emotions from readers ranging from sorrow and empathy to smiles and cheers. As I have, other readers might recognize the inspiration and encouragement they've included to ground our own lives with purpose." – *Paulette Nunlee, Editor, Five Star Proofing*

INTRODUCTION

A MESSAGE FROM
THE VISIONARY AUTHOR
PASTOR PAULETTE HARPER

Eleven Times Best-Selling Author | Empowerment
Speaker | Ordained Pastor | Story Coach Expert

Ever since I began writing, I've always loved helping
authors, whether by offering my coaching services, pro-
moting their books, or holding writing workshops. The
publishing of the anthology *Resilience in Hard Times* is no
different.

Resilience in Hard Times is stories from women who
learned how to survive and pivot in the most troubling
times.

People who read these incredible stories of....

How they overcame self-doubt and turned it into self-
confidence.

How they faced odds and climbed those mountains to success.

How they chose to use their voices and experiences to lead them to victory.

How they decided not to allow the scars, pain, and uncertainties to defeat them.

These are stories about transformation, courage, and resolve from women who were determined to make a difference in their own lives and show others how it can be done.

These women are using their voices and influence to break chains and strongholds that once held them captive.

My passion when doing this anthology was to create a platform for women who believed they had a story to share. These twenty women answered the call. Each of their stories is unique, yet they all have one thing in common – they have all been tested by life's problems, challenges, and struggles, but have come out stronger to establish themselves as overcomers in their own right.

There is a gamut of stories throughout the pages of *Resilience in Hard Times*. Some women chose to write about the pain of abortion, depression, and crippling diseases, and even death. Others share stories of mindset changes and offer spiritual encouragement.

While writing stories like these, each woman became vulnerable to past experiences, hurts, and even the fear of pulling some painful memories from the past. Yet, it's through stories like these that dreams are birthed, the purpose is discovered, and women learn to walk in their power.

Readers will love *Resilience in Hard Times* because these stories are raw and reveal deep emotional trauma and trials that challenged each author to look beyond their hurt to bring hope to so many others who may be going through similar problems.

Are you ready to take the journey with us? Buckle your seatbelt. You are about to read how these women have lived out a life of Resilience.

Your Visionary Author,

Paulette Harper
www.pauletteharper.com

RESILIENCE WHILE WAITING

Paulette Harper

What do you do when your situation in what you're believing God to change continues to say no? How do you handle the no you see every day to the promise or the word of God that says yes you can have it, yes it belongs to you, yes I will do it?

No shows up more times than the yes. From the moment we believe to the point of manifestation, we have to deal with everything that comes to bring us doubt, discredit our faith, challenge our stance and tries to squash our hope. The no tells us that our children won't get saved, we won't get that house, or the promotion or even healed. It's the discouragement that continues to pop up and the doubt we must fight off every day.

Our heart is stirred when we first believe the promises of God and when God says the time is now for that promise to be fulfilled. The truth be told, these two moments are all that really matters. Oh, but the waiting....

A mother's heart aches when her relationship is broken with her children or when there are issues from the past that have never been resolved. She prays, stands on the Word and has other people praying too. She speaks to the situation, declares victory in the midst of what appears like victory will never prevail. She fasts, cries and is constantly in the face of God. This cycle repeats itself for over twenty-five years and she still believes.... I am that mother.

I've often wondered why God allowed me to bear this cross or even why He chose this thorn for me to go through. I know everyone has a fight to contend with, a struggle that refuses to break, a prayer that has yet to be answered. We all have something that holds each of us at bay, and I am no different. My title doesn't exempt me from having my own pool of adversities nor can I escape from times of great distress.

What holds me together are the scriptures that have been recorded in my heart and His grace to stand in moments of my greatest weakness.

"My grace is always more than enough for you, and my power finds its full expression through your weakness. So I will celebrate my weaknesses, for when I'm weak I sense

more deeply the mighty power of Christ living in me" (2 Corinthians 12:9, TPT).

I've learned not to be moved by what I see or cause it to make me detour from what I believe. I've learned to block out the noise that tries to play louder than the scriptures in my head. It took me years to get here and the process was quite painful. Yet, He chose this for me because He knew I could handle it. But I needed to know it as well. You never know how strong you are until you are faced with something that requires the strength and resolve to get through it.

"We all experience times of testing, which is normal for every human being. But God will be faithful to you. He will screen and filter the severity, nature, and timing of every test or trial you face so that you can bear it. And each test is an opportunity to trust him more, for along with every trial God has provided for you a way of escape that will bring you out of it victoriously" (1 Corinthians 10:12-14, TPT).

As you move through life, you'll be faced with times of uncertainty, days or even months when hope seems shattered and moments you'll want to say forget it. But, don't. The Bible is full of wonderful scriptures and affirmations to help you get through life. Scriptures that will give you the hope you need in those very hours when the picture you see disagrees with the promises of God.

There's nothing in life that can take you out if you don't allow it. There is no test, trial or hardship that will come that has the power to defeat you...unless you let it. There is no mountain too big or hard to climb that God isn't capable of giving you the willpower and strength to climb.

No matter how many times your situation tries to look you dead in the face and say it's not going to happen, your faith and confidence must be in God and His Word. You'll have to trust Him in the process that you are equipped and built for. No matter how severe it is He can sustain you under the pressure. Remember, He has screened and filters the severity of every trial so you can deal with it because He has prepared you for it.

I'm not saying that the process or the road is going to be easy because there were moments on my journey where I got punched in the gut by something that was said and done. And I felt so defeated, but I continued moving forward. I knew if God didn't want me to experience it, He would have stopped it from happening.

A resilient person has the ability to bounce back and recover from horrendous events, hard times, and adverse conditions. That's how God created you. Yes, God created you with the bounce back, but there are some things you need to do as well.

Never give in to the temptation that pushes you out of your character or causes you to behave in a manner that displeases God. Your faith is going to be tried over and over. When you think you've made progress, something will happen that might make you feel like you've taken two steps back. This is why it's so important to guard your heart and mind from the fiery darts that the enemy will throw at you. "Above all else, guard your heart, for everything you do flows from it" (Proverbs 4:23, NIV).

I don't have to wonder anymore why He chose me for this because I know I am the one who can deal with it and so are you. If you find yourself wavering or almost at the point of giving up, here are some affirmations that will help keep you trusting and believing until what you've prayed for comes to pass.

- I believe God and not my circumstances.
- I know who I am and my faith will not flinch.
- I am prepared for where I am.
- I have been chosen for this assignment.
- I know I will survive.
- I will land on my feet.
- I know God will help me in the time of trouble.
- I know I am anointed for this.
- I am more than a conqueror.

- I know I will see the promises of God fulfilled in my life.

"Here's what I've learned through it all: Don't give up; don't be impatient; be entwined as one with the Lord. Be brave and courageous, and never lose hope, yes, keep on waiting—for he will never disappoint you" (Psalm 27:14, *TPT*).

ABOUT THE AUTHOR

Paulette Harper is an eleven-time best-selling, two-time award-winning author, speaker, certified empowerment coach, and expert story coach. She has been featured in CBS, ABC, The Sacramento Observer, CBN, and NBC.

Harper uses her gifts to motivate ambitious Christian women speakers and entrepreneurs to write, publish books, and be the catalyst for transformation in their spheres of influence. Committed to empowering women, she equips them with tools to unapologetically share their voices and stories, as well as push past barriers and discover their purpose, so they may become the best version of themselves.

The founder of Elevate Your Story Mastery Program, she teaches aspiring authors how to publish books and is the visionary author of two #1 Bestselling book anthologies:

Arise From The Ashes and Women Who Soar with fourteen co-authors. Her third anthology, Resilience in Hard Times, releases in June, 2021.

As a minister of the Gospel, she has devoted her life to sharing the message of hope on as many platforms as possible. Paulette preaches, "Live with purpose. Don't limit God. Stay focused and allow God to take you places you have only imagined."

Her motto "I teach women how to take the mic, unapologetically share their stories, and take centerstage.

Connect with Paulette

- Website www.pauletteharper.com
- Link tree: https://linktr.ee/pauletteharper
- LinkedIn: https://www.linkedin.com/in/paulette-harper/
- Business: Write Now Literary Book Tours www.wnlbooktours.com
- Facebook: https://www.facebook.com/profile.php?id=100010047302425
- IG: https://www.instagram.com/pauletteharper1/
- Twitter: https://twitter.com/pauletteharper

BETRAYED TO BECOME BLESSED

Misha-elle (Misha) Hammer

"The Lord will perfect that which concerns me" (Psalm 138:8 NKJV)

Those of us who will face betrayals in our lives are, in fact, destined for power and greatness. It is through these tumultuous times when we are given the opportunity to experience victories and spiritual elevations both in the natural and equally in the spiritual. If not for emotional trials in our lives, we would not know the healing powers of God nor experience the emotional growth it takes for us to be completely whole. The difficulty is not only the trial itself, it is also finding and applying the resilient method God provides to us for the battles we face. Victory is in the spiritual knowledge of how to tear down the stronghold of a perpetual sabotaging spirit that attaches itself into our lives. This chapter is intended to offer practical and spiritual solutions for the pain caused from offenses and mistreatments by those we have loved.

I was left emotionally bankrupt after he told me the baby was due in two months. I didn't even know there was another woman in the picture, let alone a child. A million thoughts went through my head in that moment. The worst of it all, I was being told this in a text message. What I thought was a serious relationship that would go well into my future had suddenly ended and I was in turmoil, just like that. This pain was new, a pain that I had never felt before and all too consuming. I did not know I could hurt that deep nor did I know how to end my deep pain.

Each morning after I received his news was filled with indescribable pain. This situation had not only blindsided me, it also consumed my thoughts. The feeling of pain never left me. The moment I opened my eyes to the moment I laid back down to sleep the pain was present. Pain paralyzed my thoughts, appetite, even my money. I used to be financially dependent on my ex and his abandonment caused devastation and financial uncertainty. Needless to say, I was in a terrible situation and an even worse state of mind.

My emotions were in a constant spiral downward. I had no meaningful reasoning as to why this was happening to me. It was constant turmoil of how I felt and how I had been deceived in my heart. I knew I had to get to the other side of this pain. I knew I had to once again FEEL happy, grounded, worshipping and thanking Jesus. However, I was blindsided by devastation and it was impossible to enjoy my life because my heart was shattered and my emotions traumatized. How on earth was this going to turn out? How on earth is God going to get the victory in this? Will I ever feel good again? It was dark in my heart and even darker in my thoughts. How will I ever get out of this mess, Lord? God, please HELP me!

I am a person of understanding. Peace is difficult when I cannot understand a situation in my life. My prayers, for a while, were centered around fixing my relationship. When we have our world suddenly ripped out from underneath us, we have need for normalcy to return. This is a normal reaction to sudden trauma, however, this need was not serving me. This relationship was never going to be mended back together. The relationship was not going to be the same, neither would I stay the same. God used this relationship to reveal the cunning, crafty ways of deceiving, narcissistic people. Apparently, I had many deceivers in my life and this betrayal would capture the other Judases in my camp for good.

Emotions are a very sacred part of our vessel. Our emotions are where the issues of our lives truly exist. The Bible says, "Keep your heart with all diligence, for out of it spring the issues of life" (Proverbs 4:23 NKJV). When we are faced with betrayals, we must have certain key things in our lives in order to facilitate healing. You did not cause the battle, but it is still your fight to win. Understanding this took up the majority of my healing time, but once I understood that it was my responsibility to do everything I needed to do to get into a better place, God given resilient methods began to flow.

When the pastor's affair, divorce and remarriage to his mistress came to the surface, my eyes were finally opened as to why God had me leave this particular congregation. The church was vibrant, contemporary, large and reputable. I loved going to this church until God's spirit began to leave slowly, but surely. I had been sitting under a pastor who was a deceiver himself. I thank God now that He led me out, but while He was leading me to move on, there was an internal fight. I didn't know why God was leading me out, but it had everything to do with being delivered and completely healed from heartbreak and deception from the lies of my ex.

A huge component to healing is the correct pastoral covering. Don't just sit there in mess. Recognize you need healing and go and pursue that healing. Spiritual teachings must be true, because the Spirit of Truth has to lead you into all truth when you have been lied to. (John 16:13 NKJV). The pastors I have now lead from a true, whole and spirit-filled place. No scandal has rocked this church and the fruit is there to show it. I was able to not only grow in Christ, but bear fruit myself.

Truth is what pain needs in order to be set free. Truth is what enables healing from deception and lies. We know that the spirit of God is all truth and that the spirit of God is confirmed by the Word of God. You and I will need spiritual covering that does not have a trace of deception in order to heal. On top of that, you're going to need some real strong relationships that exude the true content of love. You're going to need these honest relationships to pour into you in times of brokenness.

Friends can be our greatest support and sometimes our biggest Judas as well. It will take a true trial in your life to help you identify who is for you and who is against you. My heartbreak exposed more betrayals from friends than I had strength for at the time. When I knew it was time for me and this friend to part ways, the spirit of God was letting me know by the growing feeling of unease in her presence. When there is a friend who has contempt in their heart toward you, this relationship will block your healing from fully coming. Satan has a way of preventing us from reaching our destiny when he uses close relationships to hurt us, throw roadblocks up in our path or gossip and lie behind our backs. When the Judases are exposed, take the loss and give them to God. Move closer to your healing, which traumatized is obtained only through real love and spiritual truth. God sent me true friends, mothers in the spirit and told me to stick close to family.

The answers did not come overnight nor did they come in a year, or even two years. My healing took a solid four years to receive. The good news is that I did receive my healing. The bad news is that it took some more betrayals and disappointments in order for me to be directed to the correct path that would facilitate my pain into purpose.

Part of our victory is pushing past the aftermath of betrayal and learning to allow ourselves to trust and love all over again. In my case, letting love happen again posed great challenges of trust, paranoia and fear. Whatever area of your life betrayal came from, trust will always be a hard thing for you. With God's help, a new opportunity will come your way that will strengthen your ability to trust again. It will not happen without your full immersion in a new situation that requires you to open up and trust again. This will trigger your past traumas but also allow you to progress toward your complete healing. Our God is faithful, but mankind can be unstable. Putting our trust in God releases the burden of self-protection and self-preservation knowing that our Father is restoring us. God will begin to bless us and cause things to work for our good. Trusting in God is an act of faith that propels us to love again, enjoy life again and even trust others again. Remember "There is no fear in love, but perfect love casts out fear" (1 John 4:18 NKJV). I love you in Jesus and love conquers all.

ABOUT THE AUTHOR

Misha-elle (Misha) Hammer is a speaker, author, violinist and certified life coach. She holds a Masters in Theology from Fuller Theological Seminary and has been a featured speaker at several Christian events.

Her signature speaking topic emphasizes the depth of God and the power we have to manifest the kingdom of God on earth. She is known for powerful and dynamic preaching, spiritual insights and applicable revelations.

Her life coaching clients find empowerment and success to face difficult situations with lasting impact on their goals in spiritual development, love, family, mental health and their relationship with God.

Misha-elle's prophetic anointing is used to release seasoned and on time words from God. Her education credentials include an extensive background in Theology, violin performance, business administration and a single subject teaching music credential.

Misha-elle's bi-racial roots from Trinidad and Nicaragua have caused her to be well rounded in her ability to connect with many cultures and people. Her love for travel brings balance to her life of serving others.

She believes in women being able to provide the financial life they want for themselves. With that vision, she has successfully invested in multiple properties and stocks, allowing her to build a legacy for the upcoming generations in her family as well as enjoy the life God has given her.

Connect with Misha

- www.manifestyourdivineyou.com
- Instagram- manifest_life_coaching_llc
- FaceBook- Mishaelle Hammer (Misha)
- YouTube- Misha-elle (Misha) Hammer

FINDING RESILIENCE WITHIN

Dianna L. Lovelace

Have you ever experienced a difficult time in your life? I want you to really think about that question. Write it out, so you see it. Come on! Get a piece of paper and let's begin processing a few things. Now, let's reflect. Maybe it was an unexpected situation that broadsided you. Like a forfeited friendship, a job loss, a divorce or a death that exposed you to uncertainty and insecurity. These are just to name a few situations that can occur in one's life to make it feel like hard times. While processing your feelings, you might experience the sensation of losing heart. Cloaked in resilience, you can recover and bounce back from a devastating circumstance that knocks you off your feet. How do you get up and begin again? How do you breathe through all of the emotions swarming through your head? I've pondered the same thing. It's one second, one minute, one hour, one day, and one step at a time.

It takes intentional work and determination to cope with the adversity you're feeling.

A resilient person keeps getting up and plugging away at the situation while acknowledging it's ugly, exhausting, uncomfortable, and has left a bad taste in their mouth. Their attitude resists defeat and embodies a "pick yourself up by your bootstraps" candor. Who do you know in your circle to help you process your thoughts and feelings? When rehashing those memories, you may become vulnerable, cry and feel like you want to quit. Don't quit! Find the strength to press through the emotions. Don't allow them to control your decisions. You keep the reigns by confronting what's hurting you. A resilient person learns from what has happened and vows never to repeat the cycle again. As for me, in order to be irrepressible, I consult the Holy Spirit, remind myself *"this too shall pass"* and call upon my close friends to help me navigate through the murky waters. In addition, to quiet the storm, I study the Word of God to build up my endurance. Here are a few strength-building scriptures to add to your artillery. These are my go-tos, in times of distress with life challenges. Yes, I have them too. Being a pastor's wife, doesn't exempt me from life's valleys. Cling to this.... "You, dear children, are from God and have overcome them, because the one who is in you is greater than the one who is in the world" (1 John 4:4, NIV). But he said to me, "My grace is sufficient for you, for my power is made perfect in weakness" (2 Corinthians 12:9, NIV). I meditate on these scriptures, then apply what I've read, and it fills me with strength and tenacity to press onward. Each day will require something of you when it comes to having resilience. Now remember, take one day at a time. Don't overwhelm yourself by attempting to conquer everything in one day. Look for the life lesson in every hurdle. Pace yourself. Make a step on your new path, build your confidence from there. Can you picture it? Let's take a breather and relax a minute. Ready to keep going?

Set this thought in your mind right now. *It's going to require something of me, to press through the dark place in my mind.* The mind is a place that can stop the entire show. The mind is truly a *battlefield*. It houses landmines and potholes to trip you up and distract you from your destiny. It will tell you what you can or cannot do. It can play tricks on you and remind you of what someone said in the third grade. "You're so bashful, you'll never do anything if you stay like that." You see, that's my story. Those words came from someone who loved me and thought they were helping me to overcome my fears. What those words did was dig me deeper into a hole of self-doubt and shame. I was a very shy and quiet child growing up. I was seen, but not heard. I was afraid to speak up for fear it would be the wrong words coming out of my mouth. I believed no one really wanted to hear what I had to say or was thinking. My family was very loving and caring and would never intentionally hurt me. No one ever told me not to use my voice or be quiet in the middle of my sentence. I just developed in my head as a child no one would hear me.

I now believe that was a trick of the enemy to silence me by doubting myself and my value to God. I stayed pretty quiet until my teenage years and many referred to me as the quiet girl in the bunch. It wasn't until my junior year in high school that things began to shift for me. I started gaining confidence within and shifting my thoughts about myself and my abilities. While watching others I came to the conclusion I had to do something different to get a better outcome. I had to learn from my mistakes and from my successes. The strength God gave me through His teachings on who I am in Him is where my confidence was gained. The few trusted close friends helped by cheering me on during the race. Challenging tenacity will help maneuver you through your emotional rollercoaster, so keep moving.

Here's another scripture to hold onto.... "I can do all this through him who gives me strength" (Philippians 4:13, NIV). After you've dealt with your pattern of thinking, you'll need to check your focus. Daily, we are bombarded with images, issues and tasks that seek our focus. To coral your attention, I suggest writing out a plan to achieve your set goals. In scripture it says, "Then the Lord answered me and said: 'Write the vision And make it plain on tablets, That he may run who reads it'" (Habakkuk 2:2, NKJV).

Expect many distractions to try and derail you off the path, but keep moving forward. Remember, "The thief comes only to steal and kill and destroy" (John 10:10, NIV). The enemy wants to take that which God has given you to do and make it seem hard and unattainable.

Your endurance must steadily increase to accomplish the goal. Each day look at your plan and select one thing to accomplish. It will get easier as you gain a rhythm. I picture myself on steppingstones, like you see in water. Some are just enough for my feet, and others are large enough for me to sit and rest on. The mantra is to persist, unyielding to opposition. Your ability to withstand the adversity depends on the resilience you've built up from test after test.

Lastly, let's deal with A/R (Action Required) to finish out strong. The list looks great, you're focused, your mind-set has changed, but action will be required to finish. In my experience, I had gotten to this point and fear would grip me. The enemy would come in like a flood and pin me against the walls of my mind. I would have to talk to myself and reaffirm the territory that God had taken on my behalf. When I'm paralyzed and can't move for fear, I whisper, "It's okay to not be okay, but you can't stay." Now it's time for you to get moving and fulfill your dreams.

When taking the leap of faith, it can be very scary and nerve-racking. I say do it! If Indiana Jones in the movie Last Crusade can step out in midair, holding only to faith, you can step in faith towards your next level. I can just imagine what can happen for you with one step of faith toward being free if you apply all you've learned. I want you to close your eyes, take a deep breath and lean into your greatness. It's not too late. Now STEP!

ABOUT THE AUTHOR

New author Dianna L. Lovelace recently contributed to an anthology Resilience in Hard Times releasing in June, 2021. She is also a speaker, certified life coach, and mentor.

Dianna, aka Lady Di, is a pastor's wife and the founder of First Ladies Academy of Sacramento: a nurturing and developmental ministry for Senior Pastor's Wives. She is also one of the creators of "First Ladies Guard Your Heart Healthy Heart Initiative," a platform for healthy living and conversations.

As a speaker and teacher, she has an ability to balance exhortation and revelation from God's Word with practical application. Her approach is to be honest, vulnerable, and transparent with her audience. She desires to see people make a conscious effort to change from brokenness to wholeness and to walk in the fullness of their gifts, calling and God-given dreams.

First Lady Dianna Lovelace resides with her family in Sacramento, California.

Firstladiesacademysac@gmail.com

PUSHING PAST THE PAIN TO PRAISE

Pastor LoNika A. Harris

"I will give you back your health and heal your wounds, says the Lord." (Jeremiah 30:17 NLT). So what do you do when your healing does not come immediately? Will you keep the faith? What if your healing takes days, months, or even years? Will you still trust in God's healing promises? And when the pain continues to plague your body, are you still going to believe?

One day while I was scrolling through my Facebook page, I noticed on one site someone asked a question that caught my attention. The question: "I am considering having a hysterectomy. What are some of the pros and cons based on your experience?" Out of curiosity, I wanted to read the comments regarding that question. After reading at least a dozen comments, I realized none made mention of anyone having complications. *You mean to tell me, out of all these comments, NOBODY in this group had complications?*

I felt the need to share my "cons" with the writer, but for some reason, I could not muster up enough strength to even write what I'd experienced. I began to *feel some kind of way.*" Just reading everyone's positive comments caused my emotions to rise from feelings of anger, frustration, and sadness. I began questioning God and asking Him why? Why me, Lord? Why did I have to be that "*one*" individual to have complications from a hysterectomy? "Why not you?" was His loving response. "For my grace is sufficient for you, for my power is made perfect in weakness" (2 Corinthians 12:9 NIV) and "I will give you back your health and heal your wounds" (Jeremiah 30:17 NLT).

If someone had told me two years ago I would be writing about my experience from a botched surgery and how I kept my praise, I would have said they were out of their mind. March 1, 2019 was a day I would never forget—the day that would be the start to many medical procedures that were to come. Like many African American women, I suffered from heavy menstrual cramps due to fibroids. In fact, I had multiple major surgeries to have them removed. I had finally gotten to the point to declare, "Enough is enough!" I made the decision to have the fibroids removed.

On March 1, 2019, I was scheduled to have a same-day procedure in efforts to remove the fibroids. I was so excited because I just knew that day would be the day

I would finally get some relief and would get back to a life of "normalcy." That excitement was short-lived. The doctor could not complete the procedure to remove the fibroids because I didn't have just one fibroid, but a cluster of fibroids; they were rejecting the instrument from penetrating. Talk about disappointment. So now what? What was plan B? I decided to have a partial hysterectomy. A sister girl needed some relief, and I could not take the chance the fibroids could grow back.

The current facility could not accommodate my request, therefore I agreed to be outsourced to another facility that was able to perform the partial hysterectomy. Once again, I got excited, Like I said, I needed some relief. Now here is where everything begins to shift.

My second admission for the procedure took place on April 17, 2019. The doctors at this facility performed my partial hysterectomy and "successfully" removed eight fibroids. Notice the quotations around the word "*successfully?*" As you will later read, there was nothing "*successfully*" about this surgery. The following day, April 18, 2019, I was discharged with bandages over a wound down my stomach and an ostomy bag attached to my side. I thought my discharge on that day would be the beginning of my recovery time at home, but that was not the case. It was during this time my body begin to "feel funny." I was experiencing hot flashes, then chills that took place for six days straight. In my mind I thought menopause was already setting in, so I thought nothing of it. The hot flashes and the chills had gotten worse. I knew then something was not quite right. Remember, I stated earlier I had an ostomy bag attached to my side. In my mind, I'm thinking is this normal? All of this from a hysterectomy? Instantly I heard the Lord say "Infection."

My third admission to the hospital was on April 28, 2019, Easter Sunday. I had to make an urgent trip to the emergency room (ER) because my temperature rose to 101.8 degrees. Unbeknownst to me, my body was fighting off an infection all week! Tests were conducted and I was told the infection was from the fluid in my bowels. I had developed an abscess! I was in SHOCK and AWE. How had this happened? A myriad of emotions was going through me. During my partial hysterectomy, the doctor nicked my bowels. That day I had to have two more surgeries: first to drain the abscess and second to mend the nicked bowels. At this point I was numb. As bad as I wanted to cry, I could not shed a tear. All I could do was ask "Why, Why me, Lord, Why?" Almost instantly a calmness came over me and my Heavenly Father reminded me, "All things work together for good to them that love God, to them who are the called according to His purpose" (Romans 8:28 KJV). It was at that moment my pouting turned into praise.

The recovery time was from April 29, through May 4, 2019. And again, that was short lived because my ostomy bag had quickly filled again. So, May 4, became my fourth admission to the ER. My recovery time at home from that bout lasted from May 5, to May 11, 2019. By now you should be able to sense my pain, feel my frustration. But through it all, I DID NOT stop my praise!

Sunday, Mother's Day, May 12, I had my fifth admission to the ER. Out of frustration with the hospital/ER where I initially had my hysterectomy, I decided to get a "second opinion" and go to a different ER. The output from my stomach wound into my ostomy bag was so heavy that it caused the staples in my stomach to loosen and some came out. After tests and CT scans were taken, the doctor returned with the news *I was not expecting*. He told me the reason for the major output of fluid was because I had developed four fistulas. This whole situation had gone from bad to worse! The open wound in my stomach was secreting bowel fluid. They sent me via ambulance back to the hospital where the initial surgery was done for further treatment; this time, I was not going home no time soon.

I spent thirty-nine days in the hospital before being discharged on June 19. I was not able to eat or drink anything, only to be fed intravenously through what is called Total Parental Nutrition (TPN) through a Peripherally

Inserted Central Catheter (PICC) line in my arm. This remained the same even when I was discharged from the hospital and recovering at home. My recovery at home included having a home care nurse making weekly visits to ensure the fistulas were healing properly and the PICC line was flushing properly from the TPN fluids.

Being confined to a room for thirty-nine days can take a toll on you emotionally, mentally, and spiritually. While my spirit was willing, my flesh was getting very weak. There were many times I wanted to give up, my trust in the Lord would not let me. The hospital chaplain would come by my room every day to ensure I was not falling into depression, and much to his surprise that was not the case. He often asked, "How can you keep a smile on your face especially knowing you have four open holes in your stomach?" My response, was always, "I trust God," and my response always encouraged him.

Praising the Lord through one of the hardest times in my life is what kept me emotionally, mentally and spiritually sounded. He promised me, "I will give you back your health and heal your wounds, says the Lord" (Jeremiah 30:17 NLT); therefore, "His praise shall continually be in my mouth" (Psalm 34:1 NKJV). Two years after the initial surgery, I am still experiencing pain. I even had to have three aspirations done to remove fluid within my abdomen, but through it all, I learned how to push past all my pain, praise my Lord and trust that He "will keep him in perfect peace, whose mind is stayed on You." (Isaiah 26:3 NKJV).

ABOUT THE AUTHOR

New author Pastor LoNika A. Harris has co-authored an anthology Resilience in Hard Times releasing in June, 2021.

She is Co-pastor and Co-founder of New Life Christian Fellowship Center Texas alongside her husband Senior Pastor T.R. Harris. Pastor LoNika's heart for God's people compels her to utilize her ministry gifts as a Pastor, evangelist, teacher, and exhorter and speak messages of encouragement, hope, and victory through the power of the Word of God.

She served in the United States Army for twenty years, with six combat deployments. Now retired, she continues to provide service to her fellow soldiers as an Army Substance Abuse Prevention Coordinator.

An alumnus of Liberty University, where she received a

Bachelor of Science in Interdisciplinary Studies/Christian Counseling; a Master of Arts degree in Human Service Counseling/Crisis and Trauma; and a Graduate of Liberty University Baptist Theological Seminary with Graduate Certificates in: Executive Leadership, Worship Studies and Christian Ministry.

Pastor Harris is a mother of two boys Deverrick and Tre-Shawn Harris.

Connect with Pastor Harris

- Email: evangelist@nlcfc.org
- Website: www.nlcfc.org
- Twitter: Pastor LoNika@lonikaharris
- Facebook: https://www.facebook.com/lonika.felix/
- Instagram: www.instagram.com/lonikaharris

LEARNING TO LISTEN TO YOUR DIVINE GUIDANCE

Jana Marie Toutolmin

Do you always listen to God's messages? How do they come through for you? Do you pay attention? Do you sometimes think you know better? Ignore the messages? Are you stubborn? Like I was.

When you look back at tough times, real defining moments in your life, do you realize God and All Your Angels were there nudging you along; showing you signs of what was to come? Were you hoping or praying or just running on adrenalin? And then, suddenly, found you were pushed up against the wall having to make a life-changing decision?

That was true for me. Many, many times. One defining moment taught me three amazing things I NOW know for sure:

- If I do not listen to God and My Angels, some-

thing bad will happen. Lesson: Trust.
- No matter how bad it is, something better is coming. Lesson: Faith.
- I am going to save this one for the end; it is the best one!

God and My Angels were persistent in showing me what I needed to learn; until I finally found my way to Divine Alignment.

When I was a child, I knew I had My Angels with me all the time. How did I know? My grandmother, who I trusted implicitly, told me so. I believed her and prayed to them and they answered my prayers. My Angels have swept in and saved my life several times. My spiritual path has been interesting, with many twists and turns, and extraordinary experiences that were miraculous.

I am currently the author of the upcoming book *The Catalyst for Clarity* and Founder of the Crystal Clear Coaching Program where I provide participants with Divine Guidance and Spiritual Mentoring.

A thirty-eight-year career in academic medicine has allowed me to mentor over fifteen thousand high school, college, medical and graduate students. As Administrator and Diversity Recruitment Officer for this unique program, most fulfilling was developing relationships and mentoring students who are now successful physician-scientists practicing medicine and caring for patients, in addition to being scientists with research labs. To this day, I still hold these friendships dear to my heart. The opportunity to guide such extraordinary students through major decision-making in their personal and professional lives was truly an honor. I went to my office every day happy and joyful, singing all the way around Lake Merced and up to Parnassus Heights with Earth, Wind & Fire. I absolutely loved what I was doing!

But it wasn't always like this. A new director had been appointed. Prior to that, I was blessed with incredible directors. It was only a short time before I recognized the signs that trouble awaited ahead. God and My Angels kept whispering to me, "Leave and work for us. We are calling you into service. It is time." I did not listen. Then the whispering became louder and more often until I heard this: "Get Out NOW! Or something bad is going to happen." But I was still too afraid. How would I pay my mortgage, my insurance, my car payment? What about my health, vision, dental and legal benefits? Would I have enough money to live if I left? Afraid to stay. Afraid to leave.

I was constantly worried about what could happen. And then it happened. Just like my divine guidance said it would. To put it simply, the integrity of this new director did not match mine at all. It was devastating to witness what I heard and saw during this time. The one thing I had when pushed to the wall were my convictions; what I know to be true at the deepest level for myself. As the situation reached epic proportions, I was faced with the challenge of making the biggest decision of my life.

I was deeply committed to my students and the program as I had been there since the beginning. Thirty-seven years of loving what I do. I was so blessed to go there every day and enjoy what I did. Now, my heart was broken.

With ten years to go, I was way too young to retire. I was beyond scared when it came to money and was working twelve-hour days. My mother had broken her neck while on vacation with us, and we had to move her from out of state into our home. My hubby was laid off, and our income was cut in half overnight. Filing bankruptcy was totally humiliating. I couldn't sleep more than three hours a night. And, just to frost the cake of my life, eight of my family and friends died in a nine-month span. The loss and grief were unbearable. I was so fatigued, I could barely function.

I had to reach deep down and trust in what I knew to be true and have faith that if I walked out as God and My Angels told me to, they would stand by my side and continue to guide me.

My life is incredible now, with miracles happening every day. I keep a journal, so I do not forget a single one. I am so blessed and so grateful. They say big risk equals big reward. I have gone from being steeped in science and medicine where only facts and data are acknowledged to looking deep into my core—my spiritual self—my soul—which I now fully recognize and honor.

I did make the choice to leave. After almost four decades, it was incredibly sad and heart-breaking to leave my students and colleagues with whom I had such close friendships. I began working there at age seventeen and spent my entire adult life at the University. Even with all this uncertainty looming before me, I knew there was only one thing to do. I had to trust in God and My Angels, walk out and wait for them to tell me what to do next.

Not by chance, they led me to an Angel Ministry Program where I studied how the Angels serve as Messengers for God. I also joined a coaching program for professional guidance on how I can best serve in the world to help others.

It all became crystal clear.

I learned so much about myself, my purpose, and my love for humankind. I was shown the amazing value of having convictions. I learned forgiveness at a whole new level.

I have a freedom now that I never could have imagined before.

All this led me to the next adventure in my life where I have created the Crystal Clear Coaching Program. I have been shown how I can help guide others through the deep dark space of confusion, frustration, struggle with loss, fear, and a broken heart.

It is Crystal Clear to me that without my convictions in place, I would still be working in an untenable situation, counting out the days, months, and years until I could retire with all my benefits. That would have been hell on earth for me.

Think about it for a minute. Are you making decisions based on your values and convictions? I urge you to identify them to make decisions that feel good to you and match your belief system.

My hope is that by sharing this experience with you, it will guide you to recognize in yourself your deep desire for a life without worry, struggle, and pain. You can yield to a Divine Plan.

My divine guidance has given me the strength to stand in my truth, discover total alignment with the miracles of my soul, to be worry free, to make decisions with ease, to heal my broken heart and has shown me how to move forward with confidence and clarity in all I do.

This brings me to #3 of what I NOW know for sure. It is possible to live and love with peace in my mind and my heart. Lesson: Love! Great Big Love from Above.

When you are in divine alignment, the miracles show up. It is mind blowing! It is awesome and takes my breath away. I look up in the sky every day with a grateful heart and thank God and All My Angels for protecting and supporting me as I traverse this amazing journey called Life.

If you find yourself in any situation, personal or professional, I invite you to consider taking the risk necessary to live in alignment with what you truly believe. If you hear messages guiding you to make life-changing decisions, dig deep, discover what you really believe and make the choice to live and love fully, all out, with a peaceful heart.

Listen to Your Divine Guidance!

ABOUT THE AUTHOR

Author Jana Marie Toutolmin has recently co-authored an anthology Resilience in Hard Times releasing in June, 2021. An ordained Inter-Faith Angel Minister, she founded the Crystal Clear Coaching Program is the author of her upcoming book, The Catalyst for Clarity. With divine guidance and spiritual mentoring, she brings peace to your heart when you are a struggling with grief, indecision, a broken heart, next steps in life, and getting your "mojo" back because you're not sure where it went! She takes you from crying to smiling all the while you are on this magnificent journey to a healed heart and total clarity.

Previously, she spent thirty-eight years in medical and graduate education; mentoring over 15,000 students; guiding them through major decision-making in their personal and professional lives. Integrating these skills with her High Frequency connection has led her to the extraordinary mission of healing one million broken hearts. Her greatest gift is seeing the truth in your heart and bringing it forth in a gentle loving way.

Jana Marie enjoys learning, the study of the spiritual and physical universe, human potential, meeting new people, international travel and keeping up with her many diverse tribes. Her three longest running tribes who meet weekly are The Glam Squad, five grammar school friends; The Royal Court, seven colleagues from academia; and The Seraphim Sisters who were ordained with her on Mount Shasta after completion of The Angel Ministry Program.

Jana Marie enjoys every day with her biggest supporter and husband of twenty-five years, Raymond Locke. They share their lives with her mom, Anna Toutolmin, and their Maine Coon, Nali, where they live among the Redwood Trees on the Russian River in Northern California.

Connect with Jana Marie

- https://www.linkedin.com/in/janamarietoutolmin
- https://www.thecatalystforclarity.com
- janamariethecatalystforclarity@gmail.com
- https://www.facebook.com/jana-marie.toutolmin

I DON'T LOOK LIKE MY STORM

Tonja Harris Dews

UNCHARTED WATERS

A violent disturbance just attacked my body without a warning. It forced its way into my life and it just destroyed me. It left me with wounds that were emotional, spiritual, financial and even sexual, that tried to ruin me. My life was annihilated. This unknown disease called Multiple Sclerosis to me was just a *hell storm* that was not welcomed into my life.

What is this *hell storm?* Well multiple sclerosis, aka MS, is a rare chronic disease that affects the immune system and eats away at the protective covering of the nerves. The resulting nerve damage disrupts communication between the brain and the body. There is no known cure for this disease and the symptoms may include numbness, impairment of speech and of muscular coordination, blurred vision and severe fatigue. Lord, I experienced all of these symptoms.

I've tried to understand why God expects me to live in this nightmare that I can't escape. *Oh yeah, I was challenging the Lord.* You see fear will make you say things—even to God. I know other people have experienced fear and may have done the same thing. I just questioned God. Was this right? Absolutely not! But you see I truly thought I had faith of a mustard seed. Clearly I don't. I started searching for answers, a clue, a cure, a blessing. Every day and everywhere. Do you ever go through days that you just keep asking God questions? You know how you holler out, cry, scream, cry again, then get on your knees and say Lord, help me! I need you right now. I just don't know what is going on. I need you to tell me, Lord, how to turn my life around.

WHEN THE FLOODS COME

Lord, I'm now married with three children and three stepchildren. I have a six-figure income, a home and even a dog. Lord, I even joined church. I prayed for these things and have been blessed to receive them all. I've continued to serve, give and pray, so here we go with the question: why me? This hell storm must stop, God. I don't like who I'm becoming. I'm bitter, angry, nasty, rude, disrespectful, sad, becoming depressed and starting to look like this hell storm.

My first storm, the Tornado, was devastating. I was in denial that I had a chronic disease. What is this hell storm that is now crippling me? Oh yes, I'm now paralyzed from the waist down. I'm in the hospital praying like I never prayed before asking will I ever walk again. I'm crying out, Lord, why do you want me to spend my life in a wheelchair? Okay! This is it. The doubt now is in my head if God is even in existence. What would you start to think? How do I face my husband now I'm paralyzed. Will we ever have sex again. If so, it won't be the same. Will my husband leave me because—now in my mind—I'm handicapped? I no longer have control of my life. I'm at the mercy of others, and I don't like it and can't do a damn thing about it.

My daughter is in high school and having horrible experiences and hates school to the point she is even running away. My eldest son is in the Air Force in basic training in Texas; I need to go see him when training ends for his graduation. I'm not walking, and he doesn't even know I have Multiple Sclerosis. Nor do I want him to know until after he graduates.

I'm having cognitive thinking problems as well. I've never shared this with anyone. I'm living in fear and refuse to give my family any more power over me, because now

I'm feeling vulnerable. I already felt the non-support from everyone, and trust me, I was lonely and scared. I'm praying this prayer over and over: "Yet in all these things we are more than conquerors through Him who loved us"(Roman 8:37 NKJV). I know God loves me. I just need to hold on. Why can't anyone see this hell storm I'm in? Fear is creeping in again, and I can't handle my feelings and my mind. I think I'm having a nervous breakdown. My guilt of not being there for my daughter, my disappointment that I will never walk again and living with this disease with no cure. I'm pulling from everywhere to keep my sanity. What else can I do? I need to take cover and really I just don't have any more strength.

Well, just when you think it can't get any worse, here comes lightning. The betrayal from the church was the piece of the storm that I didn't see coming. It was hurtful. The backstabbing, lies, gossip. Man, it literally knocked me off my feet. There was no decency. No order. Yet, I still held my head up and had no idea where my strength was coming from. Come on now! You all know God will never leave you or forsake you. I remembered the teachings from my elders. When wisdom comes to visit, you will see her truth. So, why don't I understand this truth, my path, this light? A tsunami is coming now. Enough, man. Enough.

I'm now losing my home, the 401k has run out and we are

tapped out. The Last of the Mohicans is off to college and we have to put our money towards his tuition. I refuse to take this opportunity away from him. The question becomes why am I willing to sacrifice and put myself through more hardship. I probably need to be still. Yet, I keep pressing through. I prayed again, then said I'm a strong soul that shines after every storm. I believe no matter what trial was before me, I will no longer be fearful. I was given an escape from each storm I faced. I was realizing after each bad situation, there was a lesson to be learned that was good. The Lord was exposing people and truly allowing wisdom to also expose truth. The light I needed to grow. As I go through each of these storms, I'm starting to see I'm stronger and better. I survived the tornado, the hurricane and I will survive this tsunami. What I am learning is this: that people, money and possessions may disappear, but God will never leave you.

SAILING TO VICTORY

It's amazing how the Lord works—nothing how we imagine in our thoughts. There will always be trials and tribulations in life. We must never forget nothing happens without the permission of the Lord. I then need to say this prayer with belief. "The thief comes only to steal and kill and destroy; I came that they may have life and have it abundantly" (John 10:10 ESY). My dearest

Aunt Ollie used to say, "The living is for the living. You're not dead, so live."

So, I took that to the bank. Live abundantly and be happy you're alive. I then realized this disease has a purpose with me as a vessel. I will no longer give it power to bring me down. My pain will be used for purpose. I will no longer feel defeated, because I can and I will be more than a conqueror. This wasn't a revelation, it was just a new mindset. This is what the light of wisdom was trying to give me. I can now walk in it! I'm learning to obtain my wisdom.Not what is negative, but to use it as light. For I chose to walk in the light. This hell storm was my assignment.

When you truly allow the Lord to order your steps, you never go the direction you plan. Looking at my storm, I need to take control of my mind, body, and my soul. I finally realized these storms don't last forever and each storm was a trial that I either overcame or a lesson that was not learned. You see we love the assurance of feeling safe from someone or something when we need help. Especially in a storm. Building your force by inserting the opposite belief of what you're experiencing will give you strength. Remember in your hearts that you have already received what you desire. Never let any storm keep you from your destiny. Go! Claim it. Don't forget you can survive any storms thrown at you if you believe you're more than a conqueror. Keep your prayers and positive affirmations all around you, and most of all keep encouraging people with wisdom by your side. Victory is yours—even in a storm!

ABOUT THE AUTHOR

New author Tonja Dews recently contributed to an anthology Resilience in Hard Times releasing in June, 2021.

First a woman of God, Tonja has had Multiple Sclerosis (MS) for twenty years. For the last seven years, she has dedicated her life advocating and encouraging for MS awareness. In 2019 the Multiple Sclerosis Motivational Speaker Facebook page was launched on social media. This forum provided an atmosphere of love, healing and unity with current MS information and inspiring testimonials. Her personal platform is her "Daily Teacups" on social media. Her "teacups" are scriptures to be applied to everyday living and to bring encouragement to all. She is taking her pain now to serve as purpose to those with Multiple Sclerosis.

She has been recognized by the Multiple Sclerosis Foundation, Multiple Sclerosis Society, National Congress of Black Women, Luv Radio Network Group, churches, pastors, friends and family.

Tonja is a loving wife with her biggest supporter being her husband, Jesse Dews. They have six children of mine, yours and ours and seven grandchildren.

Connect with Tonja

- mystoryourstory1@gmail.com
- https://www.instagram.com/o_tee_dews/
- https://www.facebook.com/tonja.harrisdews

THE JOURNEY TO BECOMING A STAR!

Dr. Alena Zachery-Ross

Do you remember feeling shy as a child? How about feeling awkward as a teen? What about vulnerable as a young adult? Those memories are often some of our worst. The feelings of doubt, shame, and unworthiness are hard to forget. Often we can remember specific people and places that we associate with those awful times. I look back and feel for that younger self. Yet, I must reveal that it is how I felt not so long ago. It's acceptable to have those experiences in our youth, but it's not when you are the church's Pastor and the school district's Superintendent. Everyone expects leaders to have it all together. They expect leaders to have confidence and high self-esteem. What happens when you don't?

My journey to living and leading my best life and becoming the star begins with me hitting rock bottom in my career. It was the day I resigned from the top position in the high-performing, financially-resourced school district. I was on top of the world! I had achieved something that most African American educators in my area would never accomplish. I had landed the job that others had only dreamed of ascending to. I was the first African American and an outsider hired to lead this prestigious district forward. I was recruited because I was intelligent, articulate, well put together, and accepted—so I thought. I had experienced success even despite barriers and had, again, broken the glass ceiling. This wasn't the first time. I had been the first African American elementary principal, the first African American, first as a female secondary principal, and the first African American assistant superintendent in a district located in a county where white males dominated. I had persevered through threats, disrespect, and intentional sabotage. It did not dismay me. I had the fortitude and had been persistent. With God's help and the support of my family, I had finally done it. I had finally reached the pinnacle of my career.

Upon arrival, I was welcomed and had already started to make a sustainable and significant impact on the students, staff, and community. We dealt with some challenging topics: equity and identity, and the community was in support of our collective work. As a result, I received the highest-rated evaluation I had ever had, and all was going smoothly... until IT happened!! The reality that they didn't like me set in. The fact that this African American leader was passionate, assertive, and curious didn't fit their single story. They thought I didn't fit because they had a single story about how I was to act, show up, and lead.

I was shaken. I had been a sought-after educational leader for over seventeen years. I was coaching other leaders throughout the state, and suddenly I was taken back to that traumatic moment when I was in elementary school. As an only child, I was accustomed to being alone but always wondered if I would ever fit. I always felt set apart and sometimes even felt rejected. Although I had good friends, I would never be in the popular crowd. As I matriculated to high school, although I was on the basketball and track teams, the National Honor Society president, and the Drum Major in the band, I still didn't fit in. I thought it was because of the honor classes that kept me separated. Yet, inside, I knew different. As I entered the university culture, I hoped that things would change. I was on the track team and in the marching band. I was a member of the student leadership team and joined the most outstanding sorority on the planet, Delta Sigma Theta Sorority, Incorporated. Even with my new sisterhood, I continued to feel isolated. Again, I assumed that it was something else. Time and time again, I felt set apart and alone. As the church pastor and the superintendent of schools, those feelings of rejection were right in my face again. I resigned. It was over. I had broken through the glass ceiling, and instead of soaring like an eagle, I was descending and wondered if I could get back up again.

In the beginning, I questioned my skills, abilities, and my faith. I thought that I might not need to return to the superintendency. I began to question my leadership skills altogether. I even wondered if I should continue the ministry. Although my mother, husband, children, and friends attempted to console me, it was not until I went on a fast that something changed. I had been on fasts before; however, this time was different. I wanted and needed to hear from the Lord. I was focused and sincere in my requests to Him. I knew that He said in His Word, "do not fear, for I am with you; do not be dismayed, for I am your God" (Isaiah 41:10 NIV). I know that He promised to strengthen me and help me... I needed HELP! I held on to the promises and repeated them, even when doubt came. I said affirmations daily. "He will never leave or forsake me. Do not be afraid; do not be discouraged." I would encourage myself by remembering that "In this world, I will have trouble. But take heart! He has overcome the world" (John 16:33 NIV). When I needed instruction, the Word said, "I will instruct you and teach you in the way you should go; I will counsel you with my loving eye on you" (Psalm 32:8 NIV). Although these words gave me hope. I continued to wonder why I had not fit in. Then, God spoke to me. He reminded me that I am supposed to be the STAR in my life. I was not supposed to let the people and their opinions, needs, and standards drive MY Life! I am a chosen race, a royal priesthood, a holy nation, God's special possession. 1 Peter 2:9 NIV.

I had forgotten that I have been set apart as holy to the Lord, and He has chosen me from all the nations of the earth to be His own special treasure. I had finally realized I was never supposed to fit in! I was meant to be the STAR! My light is not to be dimmed. I am not to fit in. I am to let my light shine before others. He has set me apart and chosen me to show the world His glory in me! I am in the world, but I am not of the world. I don't live by other's desires. My holiness, my specialness, comes from God!

Once I understood this, my heart was opened to possibilities, and although it felt like a long time, it had only been a few weeks. Another district approached me to serve as their superintendent. With hesitation, I accepted the position. It has been the best decision I have ever made. I am able to serve with an excellent board and staff in a wonderful community with talented students. Our mantra is we are "Stronger Together!" As a result of my experience, I now help others through my coaching and consulting service. AZR Leads supports leaders by providing specific strategies to develop personal positivity—FIRST, then their teams'. We are not meant to be like others; we are fearfully and marvelously made.

If you are in a similar situation, here are (3) steps to take:

Step 1: REFLECT on the learnings that you have been blessed with throughout your journey. Embrace them because they are part of your identity. Our struggles help us grow and become resilient beings. We are powerful because our Lord created us as such. We need to live a full life with gratitude, love, and compassion. We must remember that we are an extension of the Lord.

Step 2: BE DIFFERENT. This makes us all unique. We must strive to be the best we can be. We must have a growth mindset and include the phrase "not yet" in our vocabulary. We must remind ourselves of Who created us and why. We must look inside and say out loud, "I may not know everything...but I DO know I am up for the challenge. I know the Lord will help me to persevere because He has always walked with me side by side.

Step 3: BE the STAR that you were always meant to be. Remember your power. You will find energy by being courageous and compassionate. Remember that you are fearless and deserve the best life has to offer. Go show the world what they have been missing! Shine like the star that you were always meant to be.

If you are interested in support implementing these steps, please contact me at alena@alenazach-eryross.com or visit our website at AZR-Leads.com; we will assist you in the journey to becoming a STAR!

ABOUT THE AUTHOR

Dr. Alena Zachery-Ross is a sought-after speaker, coach, and consultant. A new author, she has contributed to an anthology Resilience in Hard Times releasing in June, 2021. CEO of AZRLeads, she uses her gifts to develop leaders and teams to transform their environments, beginning with themselves.

A leader of leaders, she is Pastor of Lane Memorial C.M.E. Church in Jackson, Michigan, and Superintendent of Ypsilanti Community Schools in Ypsilanti, Michigan. A seasoned educator, she was formerly the Superintendent of Okemos and the Muskegon Heights Public School Academy System. She served previously as an assistant superintendent, elementary and middle school principal, school psychologist, and teacher consultant. Mrs. Ross began her career as an elementary teacher and school psychologist for Detroit Public Schools.

Mrs. Ross attended Grand Valley State University and received a Bachelor's Degree in Special Education/Psychology. Earned her Masters of Arts in Educational Psychology from Wayne State University and is completing (May 2021) an ED.D in Educational Leadership at Michigan State University.

Connect with Alena

- AZRLeads.com
- www.facebook.com/azachery
- www.instagram.com/azacheryross
- www.linkedin.com/alenazacheryross
- www.twitter.com/Azacheryross
- www.youtube.com/alenazachery

FROM THE PIT

Christon Davis

"I waited patiently and expectantly for the Lord; And he inclined to me and heard my cry. He brought me up out of a horrible pit [of tumult and of destruction], out of the miry clay, And he set my feet upon a rock, steadying my footsteps and establishing my path. He put a new song in my mouth, a song of praise to our God; Many will see and fear [with great reverence] And will trust confidently in the Lord" (Psalm 40:1-3, AMP).

THE PLACE OF "TUMULT AND OF DESTRUCTION"

(Psalm 40:1-3, AMP)

It was the worst day of my life. I was served with divorce papers on my birthday after fourteen years of marriage. My heart sank, and I instantly felt the life come out of me. It was worse than heartbreak. I had no words, only stabbing thuds from the pain that hit my chest. I shook my head and gave a slight smile to the server as my kids ran to the door asking, "Who was it, Mom?"

"Oh, just a man," I said, holding back my tears and looking at the floor.

"Well, what did he want?"

"Oh, just to give me some papers. Don't worry about it..."

I made my way past the kids and found my room. All I could think about was how did I get here again. This was now the third time my husband was leaving me. After several affairs, I had lost the strength to fight to hold onto the marriage any longer. We had just returned from a family trip. I thought we were trying to mend the marriage. I mean, I had found the telephone calls on the phone bill to an unknown number. I had even confronted him about them when we returned, and I saw he had been calling during our trip. But he told me he wanted to work on the marriage. I thought we were past this. I thought I was the perfect wife. I had served in ministry with him for several years. I never denied him my body even when he cheated. I tried my best to do everything he asked. I couldn't understand why.

We have a family; we have a ministry. He's supposed to know God. How could he preach and yet do what he did? How could he say one thing and do another to me?

I had lost weight. I had a good job with benefits. I was a great help. I know he worked late, but that was for us, I thought. Why am I here? What am I supposed to do now, fourteen years later, with three kids, older and frumpy? Who would want me? My own husband doesn't want me anymore. I was angry. I felt like I was a woman scorned, who had been loved at one time and then tossed aside like I was nothing. I felt like nothing.

Many times, when we go through traumatic experiences, we think maybe we've done something wrong to deserve punishment. Maybe somehow, we caused our predicament. We think, I did something, said something, caused something, to earn the place of destruction. That we deserved this forsaken dark place, full of regret, pain, hopelessness, despair. Often, we forget that God has a bigger plan than we could even imagine, because were so busy looking at the pit; the horrible place of darkness. Not all pits are designed because of something done by us. My pit formed out of someone else's decision. It presented itself in my face, and its appearance looked like death. From its core destruction announced its name. Yes, destruction has a voice.

The Merriam-Webster Dictionary defines destruction as a noun. A noun is a person, place, or thing. In Job 28:22, Destruction is given the name Abaddon. Abaddon speaks and has ears. "Abaddon (the place of destruction) and death **say,** 'We have [only] heard a report of it with our **ears**'" (Job 28:22, AMP). It is from this scripture the Lord revealed to me that destruction is an entity, that can manifest itself as a person, place, or a thing. Out of that manifestation Destruction speaks. My question to you is who are you listening to?

"OUT OF THE MIRY CLAY"

(Psalms 40:1-3, AMP)

My pit formed around me, and from its formation destruction spoke to me. The problem was I didn't recognize who was speaking. I thought destruction was my voice. It's amazing how easy it is to recognize the enemy for everyone else, but when he shows up at *your* door you can't recognize him. I kept thinking my battle was to fight for the marriage. The problem was destruction was after me. If he could destroy me, he could destroy everything I was connected to and would ever connect to. I was focused on the wrong battle.

One of the hardest truths I had to learn is that God does not force His will on anyone. As much as marriage is something that God honors, and cherishes, He cannot make anyone get married or stay married. Marriage is like everything else when it comes to God; it's a choice. Salvation is a choice, being in a relationship with God is a choice, and marriage is a choice. My husband at the time made a choice. Yes, I could pray, fast, declare, get family involved, tell my Apostle, all I wanted; that did not take away his choice.

I had to choose to accept that choice, by letting God have control and letting go of the situation. I had to trust God. "And we know that God causes everything to work together for the good of those who love God and are called according to his purpose for them" (Romans 8:28, NLT). I had to trust God enough that if things did not work out my way, that it was still working for my good. Sometimes what we want is not what is best for us, but we're so blinded by the situation we can't see. Giving God control is the best decision to make. It is in that release we can reset ourselves to agree with God. We shift into what I call "the ready position."

Destruction told me my life was ruined, but God said, "Let me have control." Destruction said no one would want me. God told me I was already accepted, and worth dying for. Destruction told me something was wrong with me. God told me I was created to please Him, not man. Destruction said I deserved to be in this pit. God told me this pit was not from Him and He has a future and a hope for me. Let God speak to you over every place destruction has sought to imprison you.

ESTABLISHING MY PATH

The ready position is the posture to be properly prepared. It is the place of agreement with God. Now all that He is fashioning, weaving, and establishing can be revealed. This revelation can only be revealed in the secret places of prayer, worship, and devotion. New things take time to form, and no one gets to rush the process. I had to learn to be patient as God revealed to me His pattern for my new life. I had tried to form my own pattern and now God had to fix my broken attempt. He had to show me what needed to be fixed in my heart and in my thinking. I needed to see things through his lenses, so I didn't operate out of bitterness, anger, and hate. I needed Him to show me who I was in Him so that I could fully emerge. The truth was my marriage ending was not my end; it was just a piece that God used to further develop me so that I could be better. It was the best thing that happened to me. "The people who know their God shall be strong and carry out great exploits" (Daniel 11:32, NKJV). God became my everything.

A NEW SONG

My declaration for you today is the scripture I based my story upon. I declare that God is bringing you out of the pit that destruction has prepared for you. That you are arising out of the miry clay by God's divine hand. I

70

declare your path is made clear and your feet are being set on a steady course toward your future. You have much to rejoice over and with new songs of praise out of your lips you shall see the deliverance of God. Many will hear your testimony and give the Lord reverence and your trust in Him will not be shaken but established. I declare victory over you. You shall live and not die. In Jesus name, Amen.

ABOUT THE AUTHOR

Co-author Christon Davis has contributed to an anthology Resilience in Hard Times releasing in June, 2021. As an emerging voice and influencer, Christon's upcoming book No More Shame that looks to target the aspect of deliverance by the combatting of rejection. It has a heartfelt burden to effectively impact the lives of those who have been hurt, broken, overlooked, forgotten and misunderstood. With over sixteen years of ministry experience in various capacities, Christon has lead teaching series for children, teens, and adults.

As a prophetic intercessor, she moves in and promotes the power of prayer. In her service as a worship leader in dance and song, she has displayed a passion to write music, choreograph, and lead others to break through in their intimacy with the Lord. As a prophetic voice, she has served on multiple teams and ministered to countless people in need of an encounter with the Lord. She is passionate about helping others grow in their relationship with Christ as well as experiencing his power through demonstration. As the founder and CEO of SheWearsPRPL, Christon's focus is aimed specifically towards products for women with the hope of helping them navigate their way towards finding identity in Christ through the Word of God.

Christon and her husband Dr. S. Davis co-lead The Gathering Christian Fellowship in Northern California. The church mission is to make a clear and lasting impact that changes the culture, builds believers, and advances the kingdom of God to establish his presence in the region. Christon and Dr. Davis share a blended family of six children.

Connect with Christon

- IG: @christondavis08
- Email: bookings@shewearsprpl.com

BEAUTY FOR ASHES

S. C. Nelson

"You be the rock!"

The last words my mom said to me as she looked through me, her eyes glazed over. I knew in that moment I had lost my best friend. I try to block it out, but the words come back to me in the still of the night, and I am suddenly there again holding her hand. "Don't go, Ma. I'm not ready to lose you. I still need you. We still need you," I shouted, trying to keep her alive. Hoping my words would make her hold on. Make her want to stay and fight for her life. But she fought her way to that moment, and I guess she just couldn't fight anymore. That was my last memory of her.

I often recalled the first memory I had of her. Even now, the details are clear. I was about six months old crawling on the floor of our new flat. Long heavy-draped curtains were hung up against a large balcony door, probably to keep the icy cold English weather out. Bare wooden floors were covered by large rugs to make it cosy. Crawling around by the door, I eventually made my way over to my mother's arms as she smiled and bent to lift and hold me close. Her smile said a thousand words, each word giving me comfort whenever I was away from her. I often day-dream about other moments between my mother and I, moments that shaped me into the woman I am today.

One distinct moment that stands out for me is when my mom taught me how to ride my bike. I was about nine years old, and I could not seem to get the hang of it. She took me outside and did the usual routine of her hand holding the back of my seat, whilst I tried to remain steady and pedal. Only this time was different. She kept telling me, "Stay focused." I was scared I might fall. "Keep going," she said. "Yes, that's it, you're doing well." Then I noticed her voice get further and further away. When I looked back, she was standing in the distance waving and smiling, shouting, "Well done! You did it!" Moments like this taught me I could always count on my mom to hold my hand through challenges. It also taught me even if she had to let go, it was only so I could learn to fly.

When my mom got sick, my world turned upside down. I could not make sense of what was happening. One minute she was fine. December, 2019, we all went to the X Factor Concert live shows: my brother; his wife and their two boys; my mom; my daughter and I; laughing, danc-ing and singing in the audience. Me and my mother had an inside joke because she always fell asleep whenever we went out together, and true to her character, she dozed off for at least two seconds, but I knew she was in her element when she forced herself to stay awake with the rest of us, she loved her grandchildren and wanted to see them enjoy the night and they did. We all did.

The next thing I know, February, 2020. The Consultant's office. "Ms. McKoy, the results show you have stage 4 cancer." A young, strong, vibrant woman suddenly had her years sped up and it was as if she had become eighty years old within a few months. Inside I was breaking, but I tried to stay strong on the outside for my mom. We even talked about going away in October and her returning to work in November. She loved being a nurse and spent most of her life helping others. But now, here she was, needing help.

As a family, we all rallied around together to try to keep my mom alive. We tried everything from various holistic approaches and natural herbs, to detoxes and soups. But as the days got slower, she got weaker. She wasn't talking as much anymore and her mobility became less and less. Eventually, August, 2020, she slipped away.

Throughout my life, I had seen her fight many battles, but this was by far the toughest. Yet, even in this battle, she remained a warrior. When she died, part of me left with her. I felt confused about where I was going in life. My identity was tied up in being her daughter; it was difficult to understand life without her. I felt myself breaking, the seams coming undone, and the wheels about to fall off. My faith was being tested. I had always been someone who trusted God in every area of my life, but in my lowest moment I felt lost. A few months had gone by since the funeral, and I was struggling to cope. I looked up and cried out to God to take the pain away. I feared I would have a breakdown, so I needed to find a way out of the spiral. I recall my mom telling my brother and I when we were younger, "When I die, the most important thing I will leave with you is God. Never let go of God." I felt such peace in that instant. I reminded myself things would be okay because God was in control.

I realised she had passed the baton on to us as her children to carry on the legacy of strength and resilience, traits she frequently displayed throughout the storms in her life. Through my pain and tears, I began to write down things I wanted to do with my life, like travelling more and moving to a new city as well as things I wanted to change and improve about myself. Becoming a more confident woman and volunteering. I listed my goals in order of what I wanted to achieve and the dates I wanted to achieve them by. Then I prayed and asked God to take control and to let his will be done. One of my prayers was "Lord, please bring divine connection and connect me with the right people in 2021." I told God I wanted to follow my dreams of becoming an author.

And here I am at the beginning of a new journey, filled with hope. Just like when my mom let go of the back of my bike so I could learn to ride by myself, whilst her words comforted and encouraged me from the distance, so it is now. She let go of my physical hand in this life, but her words still cheer me on from a distance. The loss of my mother is a tragedy I will never get over, but through Christ's love, here I am, able to share my story of how God strengthened me one day at a time. It is true, life is hard, and loss is inevitable. But you were built for this, you were built for life. You were designed with special survival traits that will emerge when you need them most. Just like me, you might feel your pain is too heavy to bear, you may be feeling weak, broken and at your lowest vantage point, but God said, "To console those who mourn in Zion, to give unto them beauty for ashes, The oil of joy for mourning, the garment of praise for the spirit of heaviness; that they may be called trees of righteousness, The planting of the Lord, that He may be glorified" (Isaiah 61:3 NKJV). Yes, you may be in a dark place right now, but troubles do not last forever. This too shall pass. There is life after loss and tragedy. There is sunshine after the rain. Though the road be rugged. There is a smile after the pain. So "...Be strong and of good courage; do not be afraid, nor dismayed, for the Lord your God is with you wherever you go" (Joshua 1:9 NKJV). This is not how your story ends. You will smile again.

ACTIVITY: Take some time to reflect on your life. On all the good things God has done for you. The small and the big alike. Then spend a quiet moment of worship to thank Him.

Now, begin to write your life out as you envision it. See it in your mind. Believe it with your heart. Meditate on your dreams and say this prayer: *Lord, this burden is too heavy, and I am sad, but my hope is in You. I submit my desires into Your hands today. Guide me to the things meant for me but turn me away from the things that will divert me from Your will. Forgive me for all my offenses and please lead this next chapter of my life, in Jesus Name, Amen.*

Now, allow God to be God. Whenever you are tempted to fall to pieces, remember that God said, "I will never leave you nor forsake you" (Hebrews 13:5 NKJV).

My message to you is, Keep Pushing Forward! Never Give Up! God did it for me, and He will do it for you. May God give you comfort, inner peace and strength through every trial you encounter in life. Amen.

ABOUT THE AUTHOR

New author S. C. Nelson is a writer of poetry in her spare time. She recently co-authored a non-fiction anthology Resilience in Hard Times releasing in June, 2021. In addition she has a collection of many fiction and non-fiction novels that she anticipates releasing to help others, both men and women, who desire to grow through their experiences and become the very best God has created them to be.

Ms. Nelson has ten years experience working in education with vulnerable youths providing education support, mentoring and encouragement. She has worked for The Children's Society Charity and volunteered in schools supporting children who struggle with barriers in reading and writing. She is motivated to make a difference and help others through the art of literature and storytelling, with the ambition to change lives nationally and internationally.

Nelson studied media communications and has a degree in psychology.

S.C. Nelson was born in the UK and is of Caribbean heritage.

Connect with Nelson

- Email: thinkspeakwrite@outlook.com
- Instagram: expression.thinkspeakwrite
- Blog: www.expression-thinkspeakwrite.co.uk

FROM THE ABORTION TABLE TO MINISTRY

Dawn L. Crumble

Our story began in 1986, I remember the day he and I met all too vividly. Me at work, he was a customer, tall, caramel with a smile and eyes that had me immediately hooked. He came in with Debra's Special cookies from Mrs. Fields. He offered, I declined. "I like semi-sweet with nuts," I said. Off he went, back to Mrs. Fields to get me what I wanted. Somewhere along the course of his frequent visits, we finally exchanged phone numbers and then our first date. I found myself in his arms and then the kiss. Oh yes, I was immediately hooked. And the rest? Well, it goes like this....

In complete disbelief of what was happening, I wondered, *how could this be!* The test was positive. He said he loved me, and I said I loved him. After all we had been together now for two years. This should not be a decision of what to do, but an announcement of celebration. We were not kids and yet that is exactly what I felt like—a little girl not knowing what to do. I would finally have someone to love me unconditionally and me love them without reservation. Someone to call my own. I was ready to make the grand announcement. I had it all planned out. My mother first, then his father, and reluctantly, we would have to tell his mother. Yeah, I had it all planned. I was excited. Me, the man of my dreams and our baby made from love.

To my surprise, it was not one baby, but twins. I felt an urgency to name them Brandon Lamar and Bethany Joy. The more I said their names, the more excited I became, and the more parenthood stared me in the face. Sadly, he did not feel the same way. He felt we needed to make a decision. *Decision about what?* My decision was clear. I was going to be a mother, but I did not want to be a parenting single. These twins had parents. And we needed to face this together.

A month would pass with every bit of continued shock and uncertainty; we still had not made our announcement. I began wondering, *What am I doing?* The thought of what would my mother really say was a constant concern that swirled in my mind. How would her church friends react? Growing up in church, a pregnant unmarried woman was taboo and looked down upon. It would definitely bring shame and my life would forever be darkened. What would my neighbors think? I was a good girl but had seriously missed the target of marriage, then baby. Nevertheless, here I was pregnant, single and devastated.

I had begun showing and I was glad about my tiny, but definite, baby bump. The days and weeks drew closer to the day of no turning back. We had made the decision, or he made the decision. I bought the lie that we would be a happily-ever-after couple, and we set the appointment for the abortion. To my surprise the abortion clinic was not what I expected. It was clean and resembled an upscale medical office. They confirmed the pregnancy with a quick examination and scheduled the procedure. The reality was setting in. I had made the biggest, horrific decision of my life—to end the lives of my twins.

The week leading up to the day would seem like an eternity. The day had finally arrived. I was a ball of wild nervousness and the anxiety of everything that would follow had me terrified of the end result. I remember lying on the table, trying to make candid conversation with the doctor to stretch the time with every excuse. Finally, the general anesthesia was administered, and tears streamed down my face. I asked my twins and God to forgive me. Hearing the screams of the other women, I fell asleep. It was over, leaving a pool of blood behind. No more twins.

He and I had our grieving moment. For him, it was just

a moment. For me, it would take nearly two years to stop the tears. The ability to go around babies or attend baby showers was nearly impossible. I could still hear the screams of the other women constantly. The abdominal pains were a reminder of what I had done. The mental anguish was overwhelming and bottled up tightly within me. Who could I tell? Who would understand? He had failed me. Alone and lonely was my everyday feeling. I had never been at this place before; it was unfamiliar, hard, and embarrassing. While no one knew, I knew, he knew, and I was fully aware that God knew too.

Sinking into depression and thoughts of suicide consumed me. Grief and shame were my clothing. This would go on far too long. I wanted my twins back. I wanted desperately to reverse my actions, my decision. I had no support that I could confide in or that would understand. I had heard of other women having abortions, but I had not heard of their grief, depression or shame. I was alone on my island. Every little girl and boy I would see brought back the painful memory and the realization that I would never see my twins. I tried sharing my feelings but was only laughed at and ridiculed. On many occasions I was told, "Girl, get over it *and* him. You deserve better. What would you do with twins anyway?" Nobody understood the levels of pain, depression or loneliness I was struggling with. Nobody.

The moment finally came when I knew within myself that it was time for me to get up. I had to pull myself up because no one would help me. I had to move on from the most painful experience of my life. I was asked a question by his father: "Have you gone to church"? I tried coming up with every excuse not to go, but he always had a comeback question or resolution. Still the excuses escaped me. One Sunday I found my way to church and that Sunday, once again accepted the Lord as my Savior. I had taken that giant step to cross the threshold of my deliverance and reconciliation back to God. Unfortunately, it did not change my immediate feelings of depression or my memory. Church always had the cutest kids, and none were mine.

I found myself teaching the kindergarten Sunday school class. I agreed to this post for my own selfish reasons: to be around what I once had and yet wanted so badly. To my surprise, my healing began with those little ones. The biggest hugs and smiles came from the smallest faces. My lap was always overcrowded, but I loved every minute of it. Sunday was my favorite day and spending that long, but short, hour with them was my greatest place of restoration. Throughout this healing journey, my Sunday school class became my safe place, a place of deliverance, a place of comfort and a place of pain. Even in that pain, being with the little ones brought a missed smile on my face and laughter in my voice.

I was progressing in my walk with God and in my healing. My relationship with their father was no longer the same. It was strained, distant and while it was my desire to hold on to him, it was not God's plan for my life. It was over and now my healing was not only about my twins but included him as well. I had become less desirable to him. Thankfully, growing in prayer was the answer that I desperately needed.

Over the two-years-long healing process, so much would happen, but I never thought I would be called into ministry. Yes, ministry, in fact, intercessory prayer ministry. I begged God to forgive me and help me forgive myself. Of course, God forgives, but it did come with a price. I remember hearing clearly, "Will you pray for my people"? And just like that, while I did not give birth physically, God allowed me to birth a ministry for hurting women. In my pain, God decided I was still valuable, and He had some women who needed rescuing, healing and restoring. With my resounding yes to God, I asked Him to show me and tell me about these hurting women. Are you one that needs healing? God allows me to feel your pain, your hurt, your brokenness, you at your point of desperation and loneliness. I am with you in this journey of broken to wholeness. I am with you to listen and undergird you. I am with you through the process of restoration. You have more than what it takes to survive. You have what it takes to thrive. God made you beautiful, strong, loving and resilient. And in your restoration, forgive those who hurt you and most importantly, forgive yourself. God has.

ABOUT THE AUTHOR

New author Dawn Crumble first book, Until Something Happens, is scheduled to be released in 2022. She has also contributed to an anthology Resilience in Hard Times releasing this year in June.

Dawn founded Women Who Pray Ministries in 2015 to minister to hurting women from all walks of life. WWPM is now represented in seventeen countries and has grown to include Prayer Intensifies New Knowledge Intercessors Summit, Dismantling the Spirits Revival and Conference, Friday Night Live and Winning with My Sisters.

She is creating a curriculum and mentoring program for young intercessors and prayer ministry directors for the local church, nationally and globally. Dawn uses her calling as an intercessor and exhorter to equip and encourage the body of Christ.

Her next major projects are Zion Girls Academy, an academic mentoring program for girls with incarcerated parents and The Revachah House, a transitional home for women with children.

She and her two daughters reside in Sacramento, California.

Connect with Dawn

- Dawn.crumble@gmail.com
- www.pastordawn.online
- https://www.facebook.com/dcrumbleadams
- IG @womenwhoprayministries
- CH @pastordawn (Clubhouse)
- YouTube Prayer Intensifies New Knowledge

2020 VISION

Valerie L. Oakley

They say things don't get better, YOU get better. I would lose everything I built in my life before seeing God rebuild, replace and restore me to *better*.

When I decided to be healed inside and out, the trajectory of my entire life changed. I went from being a victim of my circumstances to a cocreator of my destiny. I realized that trials don't happen *to* me, they happen *for* me—they strengthen my inner resolve and capacity to live out my purpose. Peace of mind became the most valuable, loving and healthy thing I could gift myself, then to others. Doors opened and opportunities appeared. Then, at a time of grave uncertainty, God replaced what I lost, and more than what I prayed for.

> *"And a woman was there who had been subject to bleeding for twelve years. She had suffered a great deal under the care of many doctors and had spent all she had, yet instead of getting better, she grew worse"* (Mark 5:25-26 NIV).

Can you imagine how puzzled the woman was? Getting worse while trying to get better? To compound the agony, those with limited understanding probably projected their fears onto her, or offered unsolicited advice. Or whispered amongst themselves about her, how they would never bleed like that, and maybe she should give up trying. Perhaps, she felt misunderstood.

I, too, spent some years trying to rebuild my life after divorce. Yet, at times, it seemed I was building a pit. When I lost my house, job, money, mobility, friends, family members, business partners, clients and arguably my mind, it was puzzling. Sometimes I caused my effect. Sometimes I had accomplices. Why was God allowing this? What do I keep missing? I knew I was created for greater. I had the markings of "success": smart, ambitious, responsible, generous, homeowner, caring mom, attends church, serves, gives, and worships to the highest heaven. Yet, like the woman, still bleeding! I had all the excuses: If only I had a lump sum of back child support payments, if I didn't live there, if my son wasn't autistic, if I belonged to a union, if I wasn't working nights, if there was more training, if they were more empathetic, if my parents stayed together, if I stayed married or had never married, if my sons had more male mentors. Finally, if he would *just* divorce her and be with *me* everything would be smoother. Lord have mercy!

One day while living in southern California, I received a call from my dad in the Bay Area. Hospitalized and receiving blood transfusions, I went into pivot mode: I immediately called off from work, explained why, then flew to Oakland. Thankfully, he recovered and thrived. But that absence from work cost me my job. That was one of two "unexcused absences," and there was no union backup. Meanwhile, I was also losing my home in the U.S. housing market crash. I couldn't refinance because my mortgage was *upside down*. Everything I worked to rebuild in the ten years since my divorce, the dreams to raise my sons in a safe, diverse neighborhood, with a decent school system and great support services for my son, was literally, swiftly, completely, upside down. I was devastated, but a single mom doesn't have time to wallow in emotions. I had to pivot and keep it moving. I would spend the next six years pivoting and moving, trying to stop the bleeding.

We moved back to our vacant home in Pittsburg, California. At least I had a home to return to, I reasoned, and my massage therapy and financial services businesses for income. However, instead of thriving, my business dissolved. Thank God for another backup—my respiratory therapy license. I landed a job earning almost twice my previous wage. My sons and I joined a church. Things seemed to be looking up.

The bleeding continued when I suffered a broken ankle in a roller skating accident and was off work for six months. Shortly after my injury, my grandfather suddenly passed away. One of my pillars of support was gone. Did God allow us to move back up here because we only had one more year with Gramps? Why did He allow my broken ankle? Am I still not getting it?

Another year went by, and thanks to the internet, I found love! I rekindled an old flame. When we saw each other after almost thirty years, it was like time had stood still. Quickly smitten again, we enjoyed each other's company like yesterday. We caught up on our lives, went on trips, outings, sleepovers, you name it. One year into our whirlwind romance, we explored continuing life's journey together. Almost ready to make that commitment, things weren't quite working out. You see, his wife was not going along with those plans, *and* that kind of battle was not mine. We resolved to sever the ties and walk away forever. I pivoted and kept it moving, and still bleeding. There had to be a reason for all of this...

"When she heard about Jesus, she came up behind him in the crowd and touched his cloak, because she thought, 'If I just touch his clothes, I will be healed.' Immediately her bleeding stopped and she felt in her body that she was freed from her suffering" (Mark 5: 27-29 NIV).

Can you feel that woman's sense of urgency? Imagine her need to drown out the noise, disregard comments in the crowd, and keep pushing through to receive her healing, especially since the conventional ways were not working. Like the woman, I had to press through the crowd that had accumulated in my life. I could no longer continue to let life's 'distractions' and 'noise' block my healing. I had to start within.

"You can pray until you faint, but unless you get up and try to do something, God is not going to put it in your lap." Fannie Lou Hamer

With God's guidance, I found a comprehensive program that helped me make lifestyle changes for long term health. I didn't know that was the pivotal decision that would change my life. My tentative goal was to lose fifty pounds, and to keep it off without dieting. I committed to weekly check-ins, and surpassed that goal. I was amazed to discover the physical weight I carried represented other *weights* I conveniently held onto. Like my limiting beliefs about what I could accomplish, and excuses why I wouldn't move my life forward. *I'm good*, I thought. However, my health coach wouldn't let me hide behind my orchestrated excuses that kept me from becoming the best version of myself. My not-so-comfort zone was shrinking along with my size, it was noticeable, and it actually felt great to release it.

Stepping out of my comfort zones became my new normal. After the loss of another pillar, my Grandma Liz, I felt I could spread my wings even further. She left such a legacy of bravery. I would try several ventures over the next couple years, such as parasailing, snowboarding, and traveling overseas. I visited six countries within two years, and was living my best life. It gets better!

I was doing well on my health program, and was soon asked to become a business partner and coach my own clients from home. I had no idea how I'd fit a business into my already full schedule. I had put that dream out of my mind since losing my home ten years prior. However, I knew I felt amazing and could at least help a few people out. Serving others would also help me stay committed to my health goals. Greater Works Health & Wellness Coaching was born. What transpired since continues to amaze me. I never imagined my personal decision would impact a variety of people I never met, that this woman in her fifties would conquer fears she hid for years, nor that I would be restored during a global pandemic. While the world was shut down, doors kept opening for me. God not only protected me from Covid-19 as a respiratory therapist, He also 'replaced' my home, but gave me double the size I prayed for! Twelve years of bleeding were not in vain. My purpose is '2020' clear.

> *"He said to her, 'Daughter, your faith has healed you. Go in peace and be freed from your suffering'"* (Mark 5:34 NIV).

If you're at that point where you've tried every-thing else to get *better* and it hasn't been working, here are tips:

- Identify and decide on one area to change.
- Enlist a mentor or coach for guidance and accountability.
- Check your circle of support; tighten it up if necessary.
- Use tools and resources available that give you structure and help you stay consistent.
- Show and tell someone else how you did it, and help them do it too.
- Repeat, and watch God restore your life while you serve others!

ABOUT THE AUTHOR

First time author, Valerie Oakley, has co-authored an anthology Resilience in Hard Times releasing in June, 2021.

Valerie feels as though she has met her life's purpose in health and lifestyle coaching. Through her business Greater Works Health & Wellness Coaching, LLC, she continues to evolve. She has been passionate about holistic health in various forms for over thirty years. Valerie's love and interest in helping empower others to create their best lives began with her own journey to optimal health after some deep soul searching and revelation. Paying forward what she gleans gives her unspeakable joy and fulfillment. She earned her bachelor's degree in Psychology from U.C. Berkeley, later becoming a licensed Massage Therapist and had a successful practice for fifteen years, has worn the hat of financial services rep during a key transition, and currently works as a Registered Respiratory Therapist. Having all of that come together through health coaching was a natural progression.

Valerie and her sons, Tevin, and Jonathan, enjoy traveling and creating memories. An honorable mention is Rockefeller, or "Rocky", the chihuahua who joined the family in 2009.

Connect with Valerie

- Website: https://valerieoakley.now.site
- LinkedIn: https://www.linkedin.com/in/valerie-oakley-b74379141
- Email: voakley.oc@gmail.com
- Facebook: https://www.facebook.com/valerie.oakley.79
- IG: https://www.instagram.com/1valerie_oakley
- Twitter: https://twitter.com/1valerie_oakley

FROM SUICIDE TO TRIUMPH

Sonja Babino

It was July 4th 2002 and my sons were spending the holiday with their father. I'd taken that morning to clean my home from top to bottom. Singing songs that brought me memories of dreams past of becoming a singer. I'd taken my voice recorder to sing the lead of "The Best of My Love" by the Emotions so my ex-sister-in-law could hear I still had my powerful alto voice. My head was spinning with all the things I could've done if I'd only left for college when originally planned.

Once I finished cleaning, I proceeded to take all thirty pain pills left over from my knee surgery. I'd written a letter to my sons explaining my decision to end my life. In this letter, I'd laid out my hopes and expectations for them as future men. I then called my best friend and left a voice message expressing how thankful I'd been for her friendship and ended it with an apology for not being the strong woman the world expected me to be. I laid down to take my final rest on this side of the sun. What the devil tried to do was kill me, and I almost let him succeed. Fortunately for me, God had other plans. My best friend, who I'd called, felt that something was off. She'd called the ambulance and sent them to my home. It wasn't meant for me to leave just yet.

Why would a God-fearing mother of three take away the life she was given?

I was the youngest of four and the only girl. Growing up in the '70s was fun and often a bit dangerous for the only girl. I had to keep up with my brothers who were thirteen, six, and five years my senior. At six years old, my middle brother began molesting me. I had no idea what residual effects this would have on my life. As a teen I suppressed feelings of worthlessness, because that is truly what I felt about myself. I walked around thinking my forehead was marked for abuse. Not only did I suffer sexual abuse from a sibling, but young boys would attempt the same. An older uncle would also try to follow. As a child, I had no idea why it seemed easy for people to infringe their sin onto me.

The residual effects began to show themselves in my behavior. In moments of my highest highs, I'd been the rambunctious boy-crazy teenager. Then, in my lowest, I'd sink into my depression and display nothing but anger. I vacillated between being socially and sexually active to being alone and privately anxious. My plan was to never give birth because I didn't want this mark passed on to my offspring. I never once heard anyone in my family discuss mental health nor did it seem anyone knew what was happening in my very own home. Living my life under the stigma of mental illness in the black community and not having anyone to talk it out with made it hard for me to find solace. Everyday living in survival mode, most my age were free to grow and develop.

Despite my own plans, God's plan allowed me to marry and have three beautiful children. I'd promised Him I would not fail them in the way many failed me in childhood. I vowed to protect them from the evil that had befallen me. However, in this pledge, I neglected to seek help for the things that continued to poke at me. I would often hear that voice telling me I wasn't worth living. This voice would convince me my childhood trauma and its rippling effects were my fault and that my children and others in my life would be better off without me.

Though my life and its challenges would have me to believe I was an underdog in this thing called life, God has shown me otherwise. While I was hospitalized after my attempt to take my life, He picked me up from my lowest point and showed me I was worthy. I can't help but be in awe of how He has kept me in every situation the devil designed specifically to take me out. My story of triumph began when I decided—with God's help—to fight like hell to take back my life. It was like standing outside of myself and cheering me on to keep going, while standing alongside the ultimate coach and the very God who saved me. Even in adulthood, it was hard to speak aloud my childhood pain. I sought counsel so my internal healing could begin. I walked around cloaked in the shame of what I tried to do, while my children were too young to understand what was going on, I knew I owed it to them to stay around and be an example of how to survive when the world around you is trying to take you out.

Recovery from these thoughts and behaviors was a spiritual fight. I clung to God's promises, yet I acknowledged the voice of the demon whose very presence laid in wait, in hopes I'd give in to his words of despair. (John 10:10 NIV) reminds me of His purpose: "The thief comes only to steal and kill and destroy; I have come that they may have life and have it to the full."

The final saving grace was that I realized I could no longer live my life in fear history would repeat itself. Or continuing to believe someone like me couldn't use my story to heal another. Thank God I am not the person I was back then. Through my painful life experiences, I am able to share my story with the many who are even now suffering in silence. With therapy, a strong support system in place, and continuous personal growth by acknowledging God as my protector, I am healed.

I overcame my personal obstacles, but it is important to acknowledge not everyone is equipped to pull themselves out from the pit of depression. If you or someone you know is suffering in silence, there is help and there is absolutely no shame in seeking it. So often we struggle to bring up suicidal thoughts with those we love, even when something in us tells us that they are struggling or we're struggling ourselves. Battling depression and suicidal thoughts almost made me lose out on the chance to share my story with the world in hopes to inspire, encourage and help someone else. While there are days I still suffer from bouts of depression, my thoughts no longer turn to despair and suicide.

My most important thought every day is that I couldn't imagine this world without me and all that I bring to the table!

ABOUT THE AUTHOR

Non-fiction author Sonja Babino has recently contributed to an anthology Resilience in Hard Times releasing in June, 2021.

With four published works, Sonja has a uniquely wry voice that shines through in her latest work comprised of various online dating stories. She has spent a lifetime writing down her thoughts and sharing humorous experiences with those close to her. It is her unique storytelling that captivates readers.

Her chosen career is as an I.T. Professional.

Sonja is committed to using her life as an example to women and men alike to show that you don't have to look like what you've been through in hopes that they, too, would be inspired to push through.

Connect with Sonja

- Linkedin: https://www.linkedin.com/in/sonja-garrett-5238761
- Website: www.sonjababino.com
- Email: sonjababino@yahoo.com
- Facebook: https://www.facebook.com/sonja.babino/
- Instagram: SonjaGarrett247

EXITING SHADOWLANDS

Cheryl Brockwell

"A thief has only one thing in mind—he wants to steal, slaughter, and destroy. But I have come to give you everything in abundance, more than you expect—life in its fullness until you overflow!" (John 10:10 TPT).

"Lord, even when your path takes me through the valley of deepest darkness, fear will never conquer me, for you already have! You remain close to me and lead me through it all the way. Your authority is my strength and my peace. The comfort of your love takes away my fear" (Psalm 23:4 TPT).

What do the Grim Reaper, an anaconda, and a mosquito have in common? They are all servants of the thief. One creates fear, the second squeezes you, and the third injects poison while endlessly buzzing in your ear. In short, they are messengers of death. It is like walking in perpetual shadow, always perceiving light but not having access to it.

Jesus offers us life and light. I walked through the long valley of darkness for many years, but I was not alone. Jesus, the light bringer, walked with me, holding me when I could neither see nor hear the sounds of life. Eventually, He took me out of the valley and now leads me in the sunshine.

Are you ready to walk out of your valley?

The Grim Reaper arrived at my house when I was merely eight months old. My father had gone to bed early. As Mum tucked me into bed, she prayed and committed my life into God's hands. She then left. Two days later, her body was found in a river. Dad found her note. She had taken her own life.

I grew up in a semi-rural setting and witnessed life cycles in the animal world. I was fascinated by death and even took a bird to school, hoping the teacher could resurrect it. I had a few near-death experiences of my own, but always there was a protective, restraining hand.

During my teens, two significant family members died. Uncle A died when I was thirteen, a kind, godly man from whom I only ever received a loving welcome. My maternal grandmother died on Mother's Day 1977. While at times enigmatic, she loved me, and I loved her. It was a tumultuous year.

The external events were recognized as being traumatic. The damage lay in the unseen workings of my child's mind. Trauma interrupts normal thinking processes. I became hypersensitive to feelings and words, some of which hurt me deeply.

The anaconda took the opportunity to creep around me and squeeze. Grief is a heavy load, especially for a child. Careless or frustrated words only added to the weight. As I absorbed these words, I agreed that I was guilty, unworthy, unnecessary, and a nuisance. Any pleasant experience was overshadowed by the fear that it could be whisked away. I lived in constant fear and the expectation of being held accountable and punished.

Those constricting thoughts of guilt, shame, and unworthiness gave way to the swirling cloud of misery, similar to a mosquito swarm. The noise was interminable. It did not matter where I was; nothing would ever be good enough. The harder I tried, the less I hit the mark, and the more people commented.

At the end of 1977, depression came. I sat at Christmas, wondering if anyone would miss me if I weren't there. I dared not speak the thought out loud. I found temporary relief in an outdoor chapel on a camp in Queensland when I again chose Jesus.

The droning inner thoughts continued. I completed nursing training in 1982, the same year I turned twenty-one. My father's gift included my mother's wedding jewelry and the Coroner's Report. Instead of celebrating milestones, I was processing mental health issues. It was a season of heavy adjustments. Enter the thought that I should use the kitchen knives to end myself. I rebuffed the suggestion and visited a friend.

Life went on. I married, had children, completed a diploma at Bible College of Victoria, supported my husband through the same college, and then transitioned into pastoral ministry. It nearly proved fatal.

We moved interstate shortly after the birth of our third child. The town was paradoxical, and our marriage felt the undercurrents tugging at us. We sought and received help. However, in working through the issues that arose, the thief saw his chance.

I was driving a large car down a country road lined with massive trees. A vision appeared, recounting all the ways that I was a failure, worthless, and a waste of space. It suggested that I would do everyone a favor if I would steer into one of those trees. The impact and speed were enough to ensure I would never bother anyone again.

"NO! I choose life! Mum, I understand why you did what you did, but I will not do the same. I forgive you."

My answer to the vision was evidence that God honored my mother's prayer. In choosing life at that moment, I applied all the training I had received. I would need it plus more.

My childhood church provided a safe environment. I came to Jesus as an eight-year-old, knowing my life depended on it. We had a group in which all the children brought a verse corresponding to the alphabet. There were also Scripture exams. The Holy Spirit was active in helping me remember Bible verses. It has developed into a love and respect of Scripture.

Service followed from the practice of spiritual discipline. I believed I was a servant, sometimes a slave. The belief was incorrect, but God was working.

A second church had a strong focus on discipleship, and I participated in everything on offer. One particular Sunday, the senior pastor challenged the congregation regarding their belief in Scripture. I took the challenge to read the Bible cover to cover and continued doing so for two decades. It was having soaked in Scripture that permitted me to speak it when the crunch came.

I was on the path out of the shadowlands, but I had a long way to go.

We returned to Melbourne in 2001 and joined a church. Here I began to discover people who challenged my perceptions of servanthood, informing me that service was a voluntary thing from a heart of love, not something demanded. A new type of counseling followed, as did the completion of several courses geared toward understanding life's journey. I began to glimpse the light.

A new season of grief was imminent, but God in His goodness prepared the way so I could deal with one at a time. Using prayer ministry, God took the effects of childhood trauma from me, effectively releasing the coils of the lies I had believed. I could breathe fresh air. The Holy Spirit began doing new work.

The season of grief took its toll. Depression returned, necessitating professional mental health care. My faulty belief patterns were exposed, at last, enabling healing. My psychologist and I still connect as those patterns take a bit of shifting, and it is always helpful to have another perspective.

I now attend another church where I am accepted into the family. God taught me to rest, and I spend many hours in prayer and Bible reading. He meets me in these early morning times, and I hear the love song that God sings over me. I soaked in Psalms for a whole year, following up with Song of Songs. I needed to hear I was loved until I believed it, then the hooks that held death and grief to my soul fell off.

God meets with me, bringing the fresh revelation of His goodness, love, and mercy. Doors are opening, new horizons beckon, which requires even more new thinking. I am safe with my shepherd.

How are you going on your journey?

If you don't yet know Jesus as Lord and Savior or have lost your way, you can pray something like this:

Dear God, I recognize that You exist and reward those who follow You. I admit (confess) that I am sinful and that You offer complete and free forgiveness because of Jesus. Therefore, I repent of my sins and ask Jesus into my life. Come and forgive me, baptize me with Your Holy Spirit, and lead me on the adventure of life. I believe that You will do as the Bible says, forgive me, fill me, correct, and guide me until the day that Jesus comes again. Thank You so much. Amen.

Allow God to love you, transform your thinking, and connect with people who know Him. Seek professional help to identify your faulty thinking. You are not alone, even when it feels like it.

Remember, the shadow's very presence means that the sun is shining. Jesus offers a full, free, wonderful life.

My prayer is that you embrace Him and that life.

ABOUT THE AUTHOR

New author Cheryl Brockwell is answering God's call to write. She recently co-authored an anthology Resilience in Hard Times releasing in June, 2021. She has a deep love of learning and Scripture. It brings great pleasure to sit in the Father's presence, awaiting revelation and then sharing it with others.

She completed a Master of Professional Education and Training to complement her diplomas in Business and Missiology and certificates in Training and Counselling. She currently uses all her skills to tutor and train disadvantaged people.

A survivor of the impacts of suicide, the recovery journey has shown her God's heart for the hurting. Consequently, her life is about making other people's better. She has substantial service gifts and uses them in her local church in whatever role is appropriate, always exploring new avenues of service.

Cheryl lives in Melbourne, Australia, with her husband. They have three children: two married and also living in Melbourne with their spouses. The third lives in Sydney. She values her role as wife and mother above all others. The family enjoys exploring and working out how to do things. She restores her soul in the wonders of nature; walking a wind-swept beach is a favorite. Gardening is both therapy and joy, particularly during harvest season. When the weather chases her inside, she enjoys books, crafts, and baking.

Connect with Cheryl

- brockwellcheryl7@gmail.com
- Cheryl Margaret Sue | Facebook
- Blog: https://heartrestorationproject.wordpress.com/

THE BIG WAVE

Dr. Josephine Harris

"Trust that God Will Carry You Through"

Have you ever seen a big wave surfer who has ridden waves, not knowing the immense darkness that he or she is about to experience in the moment? First, let me explain what big wave surfing is: the ultimate celebration of extreme waves at least twenty feet high in harsh weather and ocean conditions that take a serious approach. This was the moment that I was in the big wave and experienced immense darkness, heavy breathing, and during the most memorable time in my life.

It was the day when my mother passed.

On Sunday morning, March 23, 2008, the family went to church. This includes all four of my siblings, my nieces, and nephews, as well as my in-laws. Funny thing, this had never ever happened, the entire family at the same place and at the same time. But, for some reasons we were altogether in the Lord's house on Sunday, March 23, 2008. This was my mother's biggest dream. For all her children and her grandchildren to come to church. She'd talked about this for a long time. It was a joyous time for my mother to see her family in one place worshipping. Then, the happy moment became the immense darkness, like I was caught in the big wave.

As my mother walked into the church building, she experienced a little tightness in her chest. She headed to the restroom for towels to put some water on her face and began sweating more than normal. My mother felt more tightness in her chest, profuse sweating, and pain rushing through her left arm. Then, she fell to the floor and that was the moment I knew something was wrong. Perhaps she was having a heart attack. Her breathing became shallower, and her eyes begin to roll into the back of her head. Suddenly, I noticed she was not breathing. This is when I knew I had to do something. It was like going straight into a set of big waves, head-on while staying calm and not panicking. Easier said than done. But I knew I had to stay calm and not panic to perform CPR on my mother. All I heard was people screaming and crying, and I am yelling, "CALL 911" while still performing CPR. Thirty compressions and two breaths; thirty compressions and two breaths.... This went on for about five to ten minutes. During the cycles of thirty compressions and two breaths, I began to get tired and exhausted, and it begin to feel like I was looking at fifty-foot walls of water being taken by gravity and pushed so far under the ocean creating phenomenal pressure on my lungs.

I said to myself, *breathe, Mom...breathe, Mom!* She took her last breath and her eyes slowly closed. I, then, yelled out, "WHY GOD? WHY GOD!" I felt that God had failed me, and I got swallowed by the big wave like riding in a barrel, tossing me around like I was in a heavy cycle in an unrelenting washing machine. But I emerged squeaky clean as a mountain of water came crashing down around me. It was painful and emotional. It was surreal to endure the ride—and to see my mother take her final breath.

After that wave spit me out of the barrel, the conditions changed, and I realized that I was numbed for about twenty to thirty minutes. It gave me some time to grasp what was happening.

I blamed God for so long and wrestled with the daunting question, why? Why did the God who is able to heal all sicknesses and diseases choose to let my mother take her last breath? Why did the God who is good allow the bad to win? Why did God not breathe air back into my mom? I prayed, diligently, for air upon her on this side of heaven. I prayed for life upon us, for God's power to pour out in my family, for a miracle to happen. I prayed and prayed until God interrupted me. He told me to stop praying for air upon her and instead to pray for serenity.

You see, it was not in God's plan that my mom breathe air again this time and live. I do not know why, nor do I understand how something so painful, and dreadful and horrible can be part of God's plan. However, I choose to have faith and trust that He knows what He is doing. Coming to terms with the fact that healing was not where God wanted my mind to focus, but it was difficult. I began struggling with the very truth that though God can do anything, it does not always mean He will.

I know that my mother had eternal life, which is in heaven and at peace. And God was not willing to breathe air into her because it was not a part of his will. As I meditate on scripture, continue to pray, and choose to trust God during this process–from my mom's taking her last breath to the grief I'm experiencing now that she is gone—I have begun to understand why God did not breathe air back into my mom.

God is good.

"You are good, and what you do is good; teach me your statutes" (Psalm 119:68, AMP).

God is a good God. That is truth, and until you solidify it in your soul, when battles and struggles and pain come your way, you will be shaken. However, if you believe and know in the unconditional love, mercy and grace, and goodness of God, nothing–not even death–will make you question God.

My mom loved God. My family loves God. And the Bible tell us, "God works things together for good for those who love him" (Romans 8:28). Therefore, my mom's death is – someway–good. It does not make sense to me; I do not need to understand. Because God brings some clarity and understanding to the situation ultimately, He also might leave it unknown. Regardless, because I have instilled the truth of God's goodness in my heart, I am able to look at this horrific situation and know my good God knows what He is doing, and what He is doing is great.

Maybe there was a moment in your life where you were in the *big wave* and experienced immense darkness. Maybe you tried to understand *why bad things happen to good people*, and sometimes you try to make sense of your troubles and your pain. At any given moment, life may seem unfair and good people may appear to be suffering. But if you wait long enough, you believe, you will see the righteousness of God's plan emerge.

God has a purposeful plan. "Declaring the end and the result from ancient times the things which have not [yet] been done, saying, 'My purpose will be established, and I will do all that pleases *me and fulfills my purpose*'" (Isaiah, 46:10, AMP).

Don't allow your past sorrows, pain, and troubles to entrap you in the *big wave* from moving into the purpose that God has for you. God knows what is going to happen from the beginning to the end, and He has a purposeful plan for you. He cannot be defeated, and His plan cannot be destroyed.

I could have fallen into a great depression or even felt sorry for myself or even closed people out of my life, but I dared to trust God with his purposeful plan for me. I meditated on seeking God's desire and purpose. "*You didn't choose me, remember; I chose you, and put you in the world to bear fruit, fruit that won't spoil. As fruit bearers, whatever you ask the Father in relation to me, he gives you*" (John 15:16, MSG).

Somewhere down the line, and it is different for everybody, you find that the big wave is only at least twenty-foot high. And while the wave still came, it came further apart. Death. Depression. Fear. Sickness. You can see it coming, for the most part, and prepare yourself. And when the big wave washes over you, you know that somehow you will, again, come out the other side. Drenching wet, grasping, still holding on, but you will come out.

But God will never leave you in the immense darkness. He never left you. You must trust God to pull you out of the big wave and let him show you his purposeful plan for your life.

"For I know the plans and thoughts that I have for you, says the Lord, plans for peace and well-being and not for disaster, to give you a future and a hope" (Jeremiah 29:11, AMP).

The Big Wave.

ABOUT THE AUTHOR

Author Dr. Josephine Harris has recently coauthored an anthology Resilience in Hard Times releasing in June 2021.

Also, a philanthropist, behavior analyst and serial entrepreneur, she is CEO/Founder of Calming Minds LLC. A coaching practice, Calming Minds helps clients to connect with the mind, body, and soul, by way of inspiration, facilitation, coaching, and other dynamic mechanisms. She has proven herself to be an ideal collaborator and earned outstanding respect.

Dr. Harris 'mantra is simple: she is inherently committed to the emboldening of women, particularly military spouses, facilitating for them all an opportunity of hope.

Dr. Josephine Harris has attained a Ph.D. in Psychology, Post-Master Online Teaching Psychology Certificate, a

Master of Philosophy in Psychology, M.S. in Psychology, and a B.S. in Criminal Justice Administration. She is certified in both Teaching English to Speakers of Other Languages (TESOL) and Teaching English as a Foreign Language (TEFL) and is an Internationally Licensed Psychotherapist, proudly serving the Seoul Counseling Center in South Korea, since 2018.

Her philanthropy is inspired by the late Maya Angelou:

"I've learned that people will forgot what you said, people will forgot what you did, but people will never forget how you made them feel."

Dr. Harris is deeply appreciated member of her communal body and loved greatly by family and friends.

Connect with Dr. Harris

- www.facebook.com/DrJoHarris
- www.instagram.com/drharrisj
- www.linkedin.com/in/dr-josephine-harris
- https://healthymindsandhearts.wordpress.com

FINDING THE PURPOSE FOR YOUR PAIN

Dr. Stacy L. Henderson

"But the God of all grace, who hath called us unto his eternal glory by Christ Jesus, after that ye have suffered a while, make you perfect, stablish, strengthen, settle you" (1 Peter 5:10 KJV).

Finding safety and comfort in the knowledge that God has established me is the foundation of my faith. I have often wondered why God allowed me to suffer so much pain, trauma and misery in my life. As a young girl I experienced physical and sexual abuse at the hands of a family friend. I was confused. I was hurt. I was angry. I had a wide range of unfavorable emotions which I directed at God. *Why?* Simply because I did not know that suffering was a part of His plan for me. I did not quite understand how He could *love* me but not *like* me. "What had I done to upset Him?" was a question I carried for many years. I studied His Word, but there were times when I did not receive their meaning because of my disappointment about my situation or circumstance. There were times when my mind was so consumed with negative thoughts that my heart was closed to healing. I later learned I was blocking the abundance of blessings God had for me.

As I grew more in the grace and knowledge of God, it became clearer and clearer there was purpose for my pain. God had instilled a calling over my life. In the womb He made me "fearfully and wonderfully." When I was a young girl I was taken through a process to prepare me for what my future held. In my adolescence, He guided me through tumultuous circumstances that would lay the groundwork for my work as a woman of God. Through His steadfast commitment to my well-being, He revealed to me that before I entered the world, throughout all of the days of my life and into all of eternity, it is HE who is my constant source for everything I need. Once I received that revelation, I knew He had always been with me.

A vital aspect to discovering why God allows suffering as a component of our purpose is to look beyond the pain. God has mysterious ways, and while it might seem as though He is causing harm to you, He might instead be healing others through you. The benefit of pain is often difficult to comprehend, but it is necessary for growth and strengthening your relationship with God. While searching for God's purpose for my pain, I was reassured that His overall purpose in my life was to make me more like Him. Actually, He wants us all to be more Christ-like in everything we think, say, do or imagine. God knows our hearts, so He feels our pain. He reads our minds and knows our thoughts. We are made in His image so He knows our every weakness, as well as our strengths. And, despite our disappointments in the trials we endure, God has a plan and we must trust His plan. "For I know the thoughts that I think toward you, saith the Lord, thoughts of peace, and not of evil, to give you an expected end" (Jeremiah 29:11, KJV). I will repeat that...God has a plan and we must trust His plan.

In our daily walk, God knows how far we have come and how far we must go along our journey to be more like Him. He understands that the way is not a smooth one, therefore, He makes it a worthwhile one. When He sees us struggle, His spirit guides us in a manner which makes our challenges bearable. First Corinthians 10:13 (KJV) reminds us that "There hath no temptation taken you but such as is common to man: but God is faithful, who will not suffer you to be tempted above that ye are able; but will with the temptation also make a way to escape, that ye may be able to bear it." With this in mind, the depth of the pain or strength of the temptation that we endure is in direct proportion to the strength God gives us to endure or resist it. It is not my belief that God purposely harms us to see us suffer. However, I do believe that when trouble arises, God uses those situations for our good.

As a born-again believer, I understand that it is not uncommon for us as Christians to wonder why bad things happen in our lives. I myself have often asked God, "Why me?" only to hear a still small voice reply, "Why not you?" During those moments, I realized even more that God was at work in my life and I needed to submit to His will even though I did not fully understand His ways.

Although it is often difficult to satisfy my thirst for knowledge or my curiosity, I had to learn and accept that God reveals things in His time, not mine. And, even when I was unsure of How God was going to fix it. Why was it taking so long or what will the outcome be? The words of Isaiah 41:10 (KJV) comforted me: "Fear not, for I am with you; be not dismayed, for I am your God; I will strengthen you, I will help you, I will uphold you with my righteous right hand." So, I encourage those who are hurting not to focus on your disappointment but to tap into your faith. Rest assured in knowing God has a perfect plan and a meaningful purpose for your life.

While seeking answers concerning your pain in an effort to discover your purpose, please understand that it requires self-examination; a true, honest look into your heart, soul and mind. During this process, you will be faced with some good and some not so good ideals about yourself, so during your self-examination ask: "What must I do to be saved? How can I be more like Christ?" Once prayers are made to God in earnest and the work is done to get answers to these questions, comfort will ensue. Keep in mind that admitting our shortcomings, recognizing our flaws and taking accountability for our misdeeds or thoughts is not always easy. Our "natural man" has the ability to conceal unfavorable characteristics about ourselves from others. However, God sees all and knows all. He is omnipresent; everywhere at the same time. He is omniscient; He has all knowledge. He is omnipotent; all powerful. Therefore, we can run but we cannot hide.

Through it all, we must count it all joy because trouble does not last always. Life is not an easy journey, but when we walk with God it is evident that it is a worthwhile one. And though we are often faced with trials and tribulations, God is there to see us through. We do not know how or when He will deliver us, but there is comfort in knowing that He will. There is a purpose for your pain. Amen.

ABOUT THE AUTHOR

Dr. Stacy L. Henderson, is a Christian Educator, Inspirational Speaker, and Businesswoman. An International Best-Selling Author, she recently co-authored an anthology Resilience in Hard Times, releasing in June, 2021. She speaks four languages and has publications in more than forty language translations – two of which are in the White House Library.

A retired Naval Officer with over twenty-five years of military service and experience, her Stacy's Stocking Stuffers Christmas Charity has provided toys, meals, coats, clothing and monetary support for families around the world since 1991. She has countless military and civilian accolades.

Stacy shares her life experiences and relies on faith-based doctrines to motivate and inspire others to achieve their best mental, physical and spiritual health. She is a Dean of Christian Leadership Schools at Christ Temple Baptist Church, Markham, Illinois and maintains close ties with her lifelong church family at Little Bryan Baptist Church, Savannah, Georgia. She holds degrees in Education, Health Services Management, Christian Leadership and Business Administration. A Proverbs 31 Woman, she utilizes her Spiritual Gifts to glorify God and edify His people.

A native of Savannah, Georgia, Dr. Henderson is a loving wife, proud mother of two adult children (KeiSha and William) and several bonus children and grandchildren, comprising a blessed and beautiful blended family. To God be the Glory!

Connect with Dr. Henderson
Dr. Stacy L. Henderson
P.O. Box 886913
Great Lakes, IL 60088

Dr. Stacy L. Henderson
240 Peachtree Street NW
#56850
Atlanta, Georgia 30343

Email – Drstacylhenderson@gmail.com
Facebook – Stacy L. Henderson
Instagram – @SLHenderson007

LOVE ON PURPOSE

Donna Yates

I can't stand it. The fighting, the yelling, the tears. Please, God, make them stop!

I knew as early as nine years old I did not want to yell or fight with my spouse if I was ever to get married. You may have grown up in a similar household where you felt loved and love was present, but the yelling and fighting were a common occurrence. How do you heal from this so you don't bring an unhealthy mindset into your relationship? How do you know what you want in a relationship unless you saw it role modeled? The reality is many of us have never seen a strong healthy loving relationship. So it might be helpful to ask yourself these questions. Do I know what being in love looks like? Do I know what it will take to establish a healthy loving relationship or marriage? Do I know who I am? Would I marry me? My mother used to say, "When you go into a relationship, you bring you and all of your baggage." She was right! You bring your good, your bad, the broken pieces, your hurts, your past and your beliefs.

Honestly, God needed to do a work in me and through me. He needed to show me what I wanted, what I needed and more importantly what I deserved in a relationship. God answered my prayers and brought my first love into my life at fourteen years old in June of 1979. We'd begun dating in December of the same year. For the first six months, we communicated on our rotary phones because we lived twenty-seven miles away from each other. Though it appeared to be a difficult way to build a friendship, it was a blessing in disguise. Unlike today's means of personal contact; texting, Twitter, etc. We weren't limited to the 160 or 280 characters we could type with our thumbs. We talked about everything: our faith, our family, our fear, our desires, our similarities and differences and our future together. After eight years of dating, Joseph and I married on September 12, 1987. I married my best friend. I smile when I say, "He is my first, my last and my everything." We both felt we did the hard work before marriage, however; the real work began once we said our vows. Neither of us knew couples that were happily married who might offer wise counsel.

We knew if we wanted a marriage that would last, we had to create it, fight for it and live it. We were on a journey to be in love with one another. The first important step was realizing we didn't know what being *in love* looked like. We knew that loving each other wasn't enough. If we were going to be in love, it was going to require us to be intentional. We had to be purpose-driven in building a strong, healthy marriage. Our goal was to become an example for other young couples. That is how "love on purpose" was born.

What does it mean to be in love on purpose? The Word says, "And above all of these put on Love, which binds everything together in perfect harmony" (Colossians 3:14, NIV). Merriam-Webster Dictionary defines *on purpose* as "by intent: Intentionally. In an intentional manner: with awareness of what one is doing."

We had to trust that God knows and sees all. He has a plan for our lives. "For I know the plans and thoughts that I have for you, says the Lord" (Jeremiah 29:11, AMP). One day I was praying in the backyard and reading one of my favorite devotionals. It said, "Rejoice in Me always! No Matter what is going on, you can rejoice in your relationship with Me. This is the secret of being content in all circumstances." I thought, *Wow! God is giving us a clue into love.* Though God was talking about our relationship with Him, it is so true for our fleshly relationships. In other words, many fall in love but can't stay in love because they are not content with themselves, and are looking for someone to make them happy when the answer is right in front of them. Since God is Love, and He loves us, we needed to fall in love with Him first and He would teach us how to be in love with one another.

We could no longer rely on our parents' faith. We had to develop our own love relationships with God. As we got closer to Him, He drew us closer to one another. He taught us that it was essential to pray together and for each other. We needed to slow down to listen for an answer and be obedient to the instruction. It doesn't matter where you are in your relationship journey.

If you and your spouse or partner want to achieve *love on purpose*, you first have to have a made up mind. You have to start where you are and begin again with the intention of making your relationship work—no matter what. Your attitude must be that divorce is not an option. We will always honor and respect each other in words and deeds. What we have is worth fighting for. You may be thinking it's easier said than done. You are right! It requires commitment and consistency. The more you say what you want, the sooner your heart and mind will catch up with your mouth and you'll begin to believe it. Is the commitment worth it? Absolutely! Love on purpose requires you to be *in love* on purpose. So, again what does being in love look like?

For us it meant looking for ways to make the other feel important and special. We tried to out-serve the other by doing small things that made life easier for each other. Things weren't perfect, but we strived to be on one accord. To be in love on purpose, you must add on the next building block of faith. You must demonstrate your love through prayer on purpose. During my prayer time, I asked God to help me be the best wife I could be. I asked God to let me see Joe the way He saw him. I wanted to love him the way he deserved to be loved. I asked God to help me to desire only Joe's touch and to be sensitive to Joe's voice. I desired to be a better wife and Joe a better husband.

I took a course on marriage at my local church, and I was taught that when I wasn't happy about something my husband said or did and I desired him to change, I needed to go to God and pray about it. The funny thing is, God listened and probably laughed. He was probably thinking, "Are you done whining?" He wanted to do a work in me and change me. As you submit to God and submit to His way, you begin to change. As you change, you draw your spouse or partner closer to Him and ultimately to you. They will begin to see the change in you, and will either accept the change and love it or reject it because of fear. That is the key. God is changing you! He wants to change your spiritual eyesight, hearing and your heart. He will give you a fresh perspective. I prayed to God to teach me how to stop nagging. To listen and pray at the same time. Instead of responding, my first response needed to be prayer. I knew that was an area I needed to change. God had to show me it was a form of arguing. It was just one sided. It wasn't easy, but God did the work in me, and Joe appreciated that change.

As your perspective changes, you can begin to feel gratitude and express gratitude toward God for allowing you to share life with your spouse. Only God can make those crooked places from your past straight. Marriage is a covenant that God honors. If you ask God to show you your spouse from His perspective, He will. You must first fall in love with God and he will teach you how to fall in love. "We love because He first loved us" (1 John 4:19, NIV). Love on purpose and to be in love on purpose requires a made up mind. Our way isn't the only way. All marriages and relationships aren't created equal. We are all different people with a different set of needs and circumstances, however; prayer works for everyone, in any situation. Joe and I prayed to be an example for others, but we still had a desire to have a role model. After forty-two years of being together, God finally answered our prayers. He brought a couple into our lives who had been married for fifty years. They attribute their success to loving God, being in love and doing those things that make the other one happy. God is so good! Release your situation and your spouse or partner back to God. Ask Him to give you a fresh perspective and He will. He will teach you how to be in love and stay in love. Forty-two years together and we are still in love! We are proof positive that "Love on Purpose" works.

ABOUT THE AUTHOR

First time author Donna Yates recently co-authored an anthology Resilience in Hard Times releasing in June, 2021. She has always had a passion for storytelling and writing even as a child. This passion sparked her love for journaling. She has a desire to pass this creative passion on to the next generation through storytelling. She loves creating the most magical and creative bedtime stories for her granddaughters. It is igniting their passion for creative expression.

Through her passion for writing, a love for the Lord and music, Donna co-wrote a Children Gospel CD entitled Souled Out. The CD entitled song "Souled Out" was performed at the legendary Showtime at the Apollo.

She graduated from San Jose State University with a Bachelors of Art in Economics and Marketing. A businesswoman, she is also committed to empowering and equipping other businesswomen, mothers and wives through spiritual support, sisterhood and community. Her Voices of Healing; prayer call provides that support. Its purpose continues to be a support for businesswomen to pray together for increase and success in their businesses and homes.

Donna resides in Fairfield California with her husband Joseph. She is the mother of Daijha and Joseph and the Yaya to six exceptional little people; "Jah and the Just Be Joyful crew".

Connect with Donna

- Email: Donnyates30@gmail.com
- Facebook: www.facebook.com/donna.yates.980
- Instagram: 1blessedyayapapa

LOVE THY NEIGHBOR

Evangeline Gamble

"Even when I walk through the darkest valley, I will not be afraid for You are close behind me. Your rod and Your staff comfort and protect me" (Psalm 23:4 NLT).

I woke up early one sunny May morning and while having my time with the Lord I was complaining "Lord, I need something to do. I can't work because of this pandemic the world is in, and I am beginning to feel lonely." I've learned over the years to just talk to God. He's always listening and that is exactly what I was doing.

Later while sitting at my desk, I heard a woman cry out. I pulled the blinds back from my window and saw it was my neighbor who had fallen while getting into her car. I ran outside to help her. She was crying because she was on her way to an appointment and felt like she was falling apart. I helped her sit in the car and ran for help. Lord only knows how I was able to lift her from the ground. I am reminded of God's Word, "I can do all things through Christ who strengthens me" (Philippians 4:13 NKJV).

My neighbor and I became acquainted while working at Women's Empowerment, a job readiness program for homeless women here in the city. A year later she got a great job with the state, moved into her own place, got a dog, and life was great. I would see my friend from time to time walking her dog. Soon I noticed she was no longer working after having back surgery. I offered if she needed anything she was to let me know. Little did I know what God was up to; I knew God needed to fix something inside of me.

When I met my friend years ago, I was homeless. Yes, I was homeless and now I'm a homeless advocate. I can remember being in a prayer service and a pastor spoke to me to tell me the Lord said my ministry was not inside of these walls, and I've never forgotten. When God blessed me with my house, He placed me right smack dab in the middle of the homeless community! He gave me a job next door, where I worked as a Resource Specialist. My work with the homeless community has not only humbled me but has taught me more about the grace and mercy of God. It is in my spirit to help others.

The day I went to deliver my friend's items, to my surprise she was lying in a hospital bed in her living room. She had been diagnosed with cancer that had spread to her spinal cord and she was paralyzed from the waist down. Because my friend was terminally ill, hospice care workers would come to her home to assist her where she would be most comfortable.

That day I was given an assignment. To provide care and comfort to my friend. And let me tell you I was afraid. This was about death and dying, believing and knowing that death is just as much a part of life as living. The question is how do you prepare to die when you have faith to live?

So, it was my friend, her beloved dog, Lulu, and me. "Dear, Lord. Seriously? No, I cannot do this, Lord. My friend is dying. She has a dog. I. Do. Not. Do. Dogs. What if...what if?" I pleaded, thought of every reason and God was silent."

I made my friend a cup of coffee and breakfast, then went home. I needed to pray and listen for that small voice in my heart. I thank God for my life and for knowing His Word. "Even when I walk through the darkest valley, I will not be afraid, for You are close beside me. Your rod and Your staff protect and comfort me" (Psalm 23:4 NLT).

So it was, I cared for my friend and I never grew tired. She was a ministry and one thing I have learned is in the ministry you meet people right where they are, you pray, and let God do the rest. My friend and I studied the Word daily, talked about life and cried many times. I made sure she was comfortable. I was present, I was there, and Jesus never left us. There were days when she just did not want to talk or say anything. It was very respectfully said, and I fully understood. She just wanted me there. It would be later that she would tell me the pain was so bad she just wanted to reach over and grab my hand. She would call out to Jesus, close her eyes and sleep. Through my tears, I was reminded of God's Word, "When Jesus Wept" (John 11:35 NLT). I went home, and I cried.

It is important that when God calls us, to be present in His presence, in order to hear and receive guidance from the Holy Spirit.

Have you ever been asked to take care of someone who was dying? Let me share with you what I had to learn:

Lesson #1. Pray without ceasing.

Lesson #2. Don't be afraid of death.

Lesson #3. Step out on faith.

Lesson #4. Patience. And God had to teach me how. You see this thing with my friend was way bigger than me, far more than I could ever imagine. Even to this very day as I go through life still standing only because of the grace and mercy of God.

Lesson #5. Endurance. The months I spent with my friend I learned endurance.

I only know God gives me the strength that I have. You are going to have to spend time reading God's Word and studying the scriptures while applying them to your life. These are times when your dependence is on His Word, what you have been taught and what you believe. You have to decide to live a life that brings glory to God. He keeps us protected and safe. We all have made mistakes—we have sinned—but we also know He forgives us when we come to Him. God loves us.

When you wake up, thank Him for another day. Ask God to use you, then make yourself available to Him. Pray without ceasing. God will strengthen you. He will be right by your side; He will hold you up! He will give you the words to say to bring peace and joy to someone who is hurting. God will walk with you and sometimes He may have to carry you. This is just one way to be resilient in hard times. God will never leave you when you put Him first.

God has been my shelter; He has given me wisdom far beyond my years and love for my fellow man. I am a Prayer Warrior; my life is ministry. My Hallelujah belongs to God.

Five months from the day I picked my neighbor up off the ground, she went to be with the Lord.

Let us Pray.

Dear Heavenly Father, we come to You and give You Praise.

We thank You for our Readers and pray their lives have been enlightened.

We pray Your blessings over them.

Thank You for being Alfa and Omega in their lives—the beginning and the ending.

Thank You, God, for opening doors. Father, pour them out blessings.

Thank You for being their way maker and bringing peace during troubling times.

Lord, help them to lean not to their own understanding, but in all things acknowledge You, Your grace and mercy over their lives.

Lord, thank You for bringing us all out of darkness into Your light.

We thank You that we are the head and not the tail.

We thank You, dear God, that no weapon formed against us shall prosper.

Lord, thank You for Your unconditional love, In Jesus name, Amen.

ABOUT THE AUTHOR

Evangeline "Ann" Gamble, a woman with an air of positivity about her, was born in Pittsburg, CA, resides in Sacramento where she lives her life in service to others. Whether its ministering at her church or mentoring homeless women and children. An Ambassador for Women's Empowerment, a job readiness program for women. Ann, having fallen into homelessness and despair herself, brings a message of love and hope. A retired school bus driver, Ann is the owner of Ann's Errands, A private car service. The proud mother of six children, ten grandchildren and six great grandchildren.

Connect with Ann

- Missagamble@gmail.com

OVERCOMING THE MEAN GIRL SPIRIT

Yvonne R. Wilson

What is it about women who dislike and mistreat other women for no reason? We see it in movies and TV shows, and I'm certain we all have known someone who has experienced it personally. Maybe you've even been the one who was giving the hate and not even realized it. Maybe you did. Sometimes we're friends with the person being mean and hateful, and you decided not to like the person and not realized why. Or maybe you knew exactly what you were doing and all that mattered was you didn't like them. There is just something about them that bothers you.

What about when you're the one on the receiving end? When you're the person people hate, dislike and even mistreat? It's one thing to experience it when you don't really know the person, but what about when that person is someone whom you consider to be your friend? Maybe even a family member or a trusted individual, such as your pastor or someone in leadership? Those experiences often hurt a little deeper, because these are the people we believe should care for us or love us and to imagine them hurting or disliking us can often cripple us with an unfathomable pain.

As much as I know some would love for me to say we all fall short or to give some explanation for why women mistreat other women, I'm simply not going to do that. The purpose of this writing is to validate you the reader who has been affected by how someone has treated them and to teach you how to overcome. How you feel is important, and let's just be honest, the issue is truly with them!

Most of us didn't just experience the "girl hate" as an adult. Those experiences first began during our child-hood. We've all heard the reasons why "they hate in you what they wish was in themselves." I've heard sometimes they hate themselves, they want to be you, or they see you as a threat. If you want to get spiritual, they even say your spirit upsets their demons. Let's be honest. As a child we don't have that understanding. All we know is someone dislikes us, and we just want to belong.

It took me awhile to fully understand why women treat other women bad for no reason. Unfortunately, as an adult I can say I've experienced this most of my life. For a while it stung at times, and it even makes you question yourself a bit. Am I too much? Is my personality too strong? Am I expecting too much? Or maybe I should tone it down a bit. To all those questions, let me give you an answer... no, no, no and no!

I can remember my very first experience around the age of four. It was with a cousin who was just a year older than me. I can still remember the looks on her face and how she scrunched her lip up towards me. I can even see the look in her eyes, as though she hated me and wished I'd disappear. It's amazing how I can still feel the sting just by describing it. The funny thing is, she probably didn't realize while she was busy hating me, I looked up to her. Isn't that funny how that happens? And I believe it to be true for most of my experiences. This, unfortunately, would not be the last time I ever experienced being hated.

I remember my experience in junior high school and crying to my mom as I wondered why these girls didn't like me. Looking back, I found myself in friendships with girls I probably never should have been friends with based on how they treated me. Knowing what I know, I've instilled in my children that relationships are not hurtful and if anyone—it doesn't matter who it is—treats them in a way they disapprove of, to end the relationship. You teach people how to treat you by what you allow. I was always so forgiving, so willing to trust that I gave people more chances than they deserved.

The hate I received from girls who didn't really know me, never hurt as much as the hate that came from those who were family, friends or pastors even. Most of these people who disliked me always had more than I did. So more than anything, that is why I was so confused most of the time. I never understood how an aunt could hate her niece to the point she would try to destroy her family. Or how a pastor could hate me so much she would spread lies about me to the congregation so no one else would speak to me. Or how a cousin would be so jealous of me so much that she'd try to damage other relationships that I had. I've had friends whom I truly cared for, who were not really my friends mistreat me and turn on me.

Because I knew these individuals and once held close relationships with these people, I felt sideswiped when the betrayal happened. These people knew my struggles and most of the time I confided in them at one point or another. Again, they all had more than I did. I was a struggling single mother who was constantly being knocked down in life. The pain left me so crippled that I didn't want to give anyone else anything to talk about. The people I loved the most weren't just talking about my failures; they were talking about all my lessons. You know those moments when you fell hard but bounced back so gracefully? No one else could have possibly made it through those moments. But I learned that is what the enemy wanted. He, too, knew my weakness. I wasn't giving God any glory by being still and stagnant.

I knew I was bound when God called me to speak and write. The thoughts in my subconscious mind were so powerful, I could literally hear or feel the judgment, and nothing even happened. I also had to remember, that I specifically prayed for God to remove anyone out of our life who was not for us. I was so tired of the hurt and betrayal, that I asked God to not let anyone walk through the doors of our home who didn't mean us any good. Guess what! As soon as I prayed those prayers, I began seeing people for who they were, and I started losing friends.

I knew I had to stop giving people the power to control my happiness. It doesn't matter what they say or do to me, they don't have the authority to dictate my happiness. Because the stings kept coming as an adult, I had to make a very real and conscious decision to be okay with people not liking me. I put my hurt in the hands of the Lord and I let go, even if I had to do so multiple times.

I was also willing to walk away from anyone who didn't treat me how I deserved to be treated. I had to remember these ladies didn't control my destiny, and God still had a plan for me even before I was created. So, when these ladies had the "you can't sit with us mentality," I had to know that I was building my own table and other ladies were allowed a seat at my table.

I also realized that it was all about the quality of the friendships not the quantity. You only need a few quality friendships. I had to be okay with not receiving an apology because forgiveness is all about you, not them. They say holding on to bitterness is like drinking poison and expecting the other person to die. It's just not going to happen. There were even times when I thought the relationship was salvageable and I would go to the person with the offense. The Bible says, "If your brother or sister sins, go and point out their fault between the two of you, if they listen to you, you have won them over" (Matthew 18:15, NIV).

Be prepared that not all people are mature enough to accept responsibility for their behavior. But I believe if they truly value the relationship, then they will accept how they made you feel. Here's the thing: when you tell someone they hurt you, they don't get to say they didn't. Finally, **Wake up every day and like yourself.** One of the best things I heard came from motivational speaker Lisa Nichols who said, "First of all, I woke up and liked myself this morning, so your like is extra."

God called you to stand out. You are not made to fit in, so we're not going to try and start now.

Be all of you, sis, you got this!

ABOUT THE AUTHOR

Author Yvonne Wilson has written several short stories and contributed to an anthology Resilience in Hard Times releasing in June, 2021. A busy writer, she has a children's book that she is publishing this year along with a biography that she will have completed this Spring. Yvonne believes that every lesson has been something she shares with others so they, too, know that they will make it through.

A single mother advocate and ministry leader, she is a women empowerment coach and speaker. She considers herself to be an advocate for youth and anyone who has had their voice taken away from them

Yvonne has a "you can sit with us" mentality and believes everyone has a special gift to offer the world. Sometimes it takes a bit of pain or trial and error to figure it. But with

God, some coaching and the right leadership you can figure it out.

Connect with Yvonne

- Email: Info@iamyvonnewilson
- Twitter: iamyvonnewilson
- Instagram: iamyvonnewilson
- Website: iamyvonnewilson.com

SHATTERED HEART

Marilyn Williams-Jerrels

Have you ever had a heartbreaking loss that shook you to your core? Well, I have. This was not my first go-round with having my heart broken. It was, however, the first time I thought I would not survive it. What was just barely three years sometimes feels like a lifetime ago, while also feeling like it was yesterday. I call it the "unpredictability of grief."

Providence had once again brought a sibling to the West Coast. Daily calls and texts, along with the occasional 800-mile visit, made us virtually inseparable once again. We had an awful lot in common with each other, including our careers and our personal experiences with special needs children. We had our differences. Yet, when our views clashed, our love and respect for one another never wavered. We would each argue our point in hopes that the other would understand or maybe even change their viewpoint. She was the person *who kept it one hundred.* To be totally transparent, going this far down memory lane is painful. I digress though, so for now, I will just go back to the day when I was told that surgical interventions had been unsuccessful, and worse. I sat with the knowledge that I had extraordinarily little time left to say "good-bye" to my best friend. My sister, "Di." Now, if you are tempted to get super pious and say that "Jesus is supposed to be our best friend," hold your peace. For truly—on this earth—at that point in time, Di was my closest friend. Besides, it is important that we have close earthly friends.

So, that day, following the conference call with family and physicians, my heart broke. It shattered. I remember at some point feeling the burning in my eyes as tears poured out. No matter how many tears I washed away and down the shower drain, more would appear. Sobbing quietly, I remember telling God I simply did not know how to live without my sister. Being that she was three years older, she had always been in my life. Di was having difficulty vocally as a result of esophageal cancer and its treatment. I had already been struggling with the fact we had not spoken for far too long. Pouring my heart out to God, I said, "I don't know how to live without her. I'm trusting You to help me because this is something, I won't be able to orchestrate a fix for."

Lest you think I had no other family support; nothing could be further from the truth. Yet, I instinctively knew my shattered heart would require supernatural intervention. So, in my usual fashion, I pulled myself together as much as possible and planned the trip, including my husband, and youngest daughter, from Stockton, California to the hospital in Seattle, Washington. As I sit here writing this today, I am unclear about how we got there. I know we must have driven. However, I do not remember anything about the trip there. Just that it was raining and cold in Seattle and I wanted no part of why we were there.

Even though I am a woman of deep abiding faith, there was a part of me that harbored some doubt in God. After all my sister had fully trusted Him to see her through this to the other side of wellness. She had also entrusted me with certain medical decisions. I was doubting God and myself because it simply was not supposed to turn out this way! Please do not miss this point: *as much as I trusted, there was still room for doubt.* I kept praying for the miracle I now knew was not going to occur because—for me—reality was an indictment against God. How could He not heal her and how could He put me in this position to make this decision? None of us envisioned it ending like this!

Matthew 17:20 refers to "mustard seed" faith and what faith that *small* can accomplish. I am fully aware that our faith is supposed to grow and not stay tiny, yet, all I had at the time was mustard seed faith I very honestly and unashamedly acknowledged to God that I was operating out of *barely holding on* faith. Yet, I was trusting that it would be sufficient.

I had learned years ago there is no order to grief. There are various stages with varying degrees, but it follows its own chaotic path. Along with my anger and disappointment, I was weary. This two year—arduous journey—had left us with extreme physical and emotional fatigue. We all felt it. And, since "goodbye" was only part of the process, I was now selfishly grateful to temporarily relinquish my role as the major decision maker. So, we "held it together" to empty and clean her apartment in Silverdale and plan her celebration of life services. Three months later, we traveled "home" to Detroit, Michigan for the services. I do not remember much of what I said for the eulogy, but I do recall my wonderful family pitching in wherever they could. I am blessed to have a family that pulls together in crisis. I smile when I see how my nieces and nephews are surviving and thriving. My sister would be extremely proud of them.

I pieced together lessons learned from this and other experiences with grief. Although I believe each point is important, I share them in no order of significance. Hopefully, they will be of benefit to someone.

- There is strength in community.
- My mother—who was ninety years old at the time—flew out with family from Huntsville,

Alabama. I gained such strength just watching Momma sit at her daughter's bedside. Whether holding her hand, singing with us, or just sitting quietly playing on her tablet, Mom's strength helped me. With each family member who arrived, before and after, I gained strength. Not only was my strength increased, but so was my faith. If those around me were *holding on*, so could I.

- You are not God.
- In the process of traveling back and forth and making myself available to assist, etc., I forgot that I was not ultimately in charge. I thought if I did all the right things and helped to make the "right" medical decisions, everything would work out. I ran myself ragged believing that a positive outcome depended on me. Sidebar: being totally honest, I realized that I learned much of this erroneous behavior from "religious circles." I now understand that doing for others to the detriment of self or immediate family does not increase your chances for Heaven. The word *no* is not necessarily an indicator a person is uncommitted, or unmotivated. I am learning to move when it is right for me, not because it feels right for others. Do not bow to the pressure to do it all. Stop trying to be God to and for others.

171

- Protect your Mental Health.
- I vividly recall seeing my sad eyes reflected in the mirror. Upon my return from Detroit, I took advantage of individual counseling and participated in group sessions. It was necessary and helpful. Unfortunately, many people do not realize that our brains need attention as much as the rest of our body does. Health encompasses, physical, mental/emotional, and spiritual. If any of these are out of sync, you are not *in health*. Believers are counseled to be balanced individuals. Therefore, we should not neglect our mental health.
- Breathing is vital.
- It might also surprise you to know that people forget to do something so basic. Grief can hit you so hard that the wind is knocked out of you. When you experience it, you may need to remind yourself to take deep breaths. "Just Breathe." I spent the remaining months of that year reminding myself to breathe. I decided not to take on any tasks that were not vital to our well-being or in some way fun for me. Taking baby steps, I learned how to breathe again.
- You can Trust God.

I had no clue about how God was going to help me survive, but I had faith that I would be carried. When I had no strength to carry myself, I was carried. When I had almost nothing to give to God, I was still carried. I was reminded that: God can handle your fear, disappointment, anger, tiny faith and more. Hebrews 11:1-2 NIV says, "Now faith is confidence in what we hope for and assurance about what we do not see. This is what the ancients were commended for."

I cannot begin to tell you how much I miss my sister. At times, I still find myself waiting for her call. That is the reality of grief. However, these days, my eyes smile again and my heart, though scarred, is mended.

ABOUT THE AUTHOR

Marilyn Williams-Jerrels wrote poetry even as a child. She uses spoken word poetry to tell stories and express deep emotions. She has enjoyed utilizing her literary skills for various organizational communications: newsletters, official letters and social media postings. Co-authoring an anthology, Resilience in Hard Times, is her first work as a published author to be released June, 2021. She is simultaneously putting the finishing touches on her first solo project, a collection of poetry.

She is a United States Navy Veteran (Corpsman/ORT), LVN, and full-time family caregiver. Her "gifts of healing" flow via uplifting words or through service to others.

Marilyn has helped to establish and maintain a social media presence for a variety of entities and individuals.

Her hobbies include roller skating, music, photography and technology.

A native of Detroit, Michigan, Marilyn currently resides in Stockton, California, and has been married thirty-plus years to her husband, Barry. Together they have a beautifully blended family of three daughters, five grandchildren and one great grandchild.

Connect with Marilyn

- Email: mwilliams.jerrels@gmail.com
- You Tube: https://www.youtube.com/channel/UC8xxsYe24_XhL-DAHgQRvew
- Face Book: https://www.facebook.com/1MaWJ

PERFECT TIMING

Wandah Mitchell Parenti

"When the time is right, I, The Lord, will make it happen"

Isaiah 60:22, NLT

I've often heard when you are hunting, timing is everything. The thing about that though is timing can go either way. You can have good timing or bad timing. For those who love to hunt, I believe that not only does your prey need to be in season, but you have to be in the right place at precisely the right time. In the perfect position, having your arrow drawn back and ready to release it at the exact moment necessary to hit your target, thereby ultimately claiming your trophy. That would be good timing for the hunter, not good for the hunted. Believe me, I've been there: the completely unsuspecting prey being targeted, primed for the hunt and ultimately struck down by the hunter. The only difference is there was no victory lap for the hunter in this story, no notch in his belt, no mount for his wall. It was simply not my time. I was wounded, but I got back up to live and to tell this story because only God's timing matters. His timing is perfect for you.

Back in November, 2000, I was getting to a point where I was ready to forge forward and get my life back after a horrible breakup. That was just about the time he showed up. I suppose I was ripe for the picking. I thought I was ready, but I now know that was very far from the truth. It's one thing to believe you are over a bad breakup. It's another thing entirely to be healed from one. There is a difference. My advice would be to make sure healing has been achieved. Starting a relationship before healing has taken place can be quite costly.

It was just past noon and I was feeling a bit famished. I called down to Johnny's restaurant to order my lunch. Ten minutes later I was off to retrieve my lunch. It was the usual lunch crowd except for an unfamiliar presence sitting at the counter—a gentleman staring at me. I felt like I couldn't move, not to mention turn around and face him. From the corner of my eye, I could see him sitting there with a devilish smile on his face, watching my every move. Little did I know he was plotting, like the big bad wolf, how he would strategically whisk me off my feet and convince me that he was my Prince Charming coming to take me away from all of my woes, then when I least expected, he would swallow me whole. I started feeling embarrassed and I just wanted to quickly run out of the restaurant.

Of course as I turned to leave, we finally locked eyes and shared pleasantries. He wore a beautiful smile. This certain sparkle in his eyes said he liked what he saw.

I headed back to my office feeling good about myself. I remember thinking, *You still got it, girl.* It didn't occur to me our very brief encounter would be more than just that, a brief encounter. I was quite ill-prepared for what would happen next. I went back to work as usual and he went to work as usual, too, but on me. I would be the next victim to fall into his trap and he wasted no time.

I was so enthralled with the holiday cheer, feeling happy about still having that *look*. I didn't even see him when he entered the store. A team member alerted me that I had a visitor. I looked up and I saw him perusing the store, pretending to be shopping. Why was he here? My heart began racing and I immediately began blushing like a schoolgirl. After checking myself in the mirror half a dozen times, I met him downstairs. Again, he was staring at me. His eyes pierced right through me, like he could see everything about me. Every single broken piece. *Was he here shopping for his wife? Or a girlfriend?*

No, he was definitely here for me. Of all the catches that were in the mall that day, he made me his prime target. He said all the right things, made all of the right moves. He was smart. Smooth, and very good at this game. I was naive and thirsty, longing for attention, love and validation and he so kindly obliged. Contemplating a relationship with someone when you are thirsty is like going to the grocery store when you are hungry. It's never a good idea. You'll end up spending way more than necessary. Before the end of that day we'd exchanged numbers and were engrossed in conversation that went well into the early hours of the next morning. He learned more about me in those twenty-four hours than I knew about myself.

My father and the men after him had left me heartbroken, scarred, alone and desperate. He rushed in like an EMT medic to mend my broken heart, take care of me and to protect me. I was instantly caught up in his intoxicating charms. It looked like love or at least I wanted it to. My defenses were down. I was blind, but everyone else could see him for who he truly was. I could not see what everyone else was seeing in him. I believed his lies, made excuses for his crazy jealousy and dangerous possessiveness. I considered myself to be an extremely intelligent woman. Loving, hardworking, beautiful, but now I found myself second-guessing everything I thought I knew about myself.

A single moment was all it took for me to believe completely in him and not trust myself, my instincts or GOD. He exploited my every weakness, and he tormented and drained my spirit and my soul. He abused my body and altered my mind. I found myself powerless. That is a scary place to be. I honestly thought I might not make it through this, but just before he was about to draw back his bow and take his best shot, I took my best shot.

I decided that I was going to get my life back. I was going to live and not die. I went to church, and I prayed and asked the Lord to forgive me. I told Jesus if He delivered me from this, I would wait for Him to send me the person that He had for me. I told him that I would trust Him and His plan for my life. He does have one. Jeremiah 29:11 NLT says, "'For I know the plans I have for you,' says the Lord, 'They are plans for good and not for disaster, to give you a future and a hope.'" So when you feel that the walls are closing in, there seems to be no way of escape and you feel your time is up, put your hands in God's hands and don't ever let go. It tells us in Psalms 37:4 NLT to, "Take delight in the Lord and He will give you the desires of your heart." Also, Prey is not who we are, rather prayer is what we do. So do that, a lot. When you feel weak and powerless, let God be your strength. Ask Him to cover you and hide you with His wings just like in Psalm 91:4, NLT, says, "He will cover you with His feathers, He will shelter you with His wings. His faithful promises are your armor and protection."

This can happen to us all, fall victim and be hunted down, devoured any given day or time. The hunter can easily sense when you are thirsty, desperate and weak.

These are characteristics of an easy kill, perfect timing for him or at least he thinks. God says in 2 Corinthians 12:9 (NLT), "Each time He said, My grace is all you need. My power works best in weakness." And remember, God's timing matters. He has perfect timing.

ABOUT THE AUTHOR

New author, Wandah Mitchell Parenti, is a co-author in the anthology Resilience In Hard Times releasing in June 2021.

Wandah, a native of California, was born in the San Francisco Bay Area but she was raised in Inglewood, California. Her true passion is ministering and mentoring women which she has been purposefully fulfilling for several years. After she completed her ministerial studies, she felt it was time to apply her faith and she currently volunteers as a counselor and educator for the PACE Program for post abortive women at Valley Pregnancy Center in Pleasanton, California as well as serves as a faith based crisis counselor for NAMI Contra Costa.

Wandah and her husband of eighteen years are the proud

parents of four beautiful children and seven grandchildren who affectionately know her as "Mimi".

Connect with Wandah

- www.wandahparenti.com
- Instagram – Facebook – Twitter
- @wandahparentiauthor